SpringerBriefs in Computer Science

Series Editors
Stan Zdonik
Peng Ning
Shashi Shekhar
Jonathan Katz
Xindong Wu
Lakhmi C. Jain
David Padua
Xuemin Shen
Borko Furht
VS Subrahmanian

T0184445

For further volumes
http://www.springer.com/series/10028

Asaf Shabtai • Yuval Elovici • Lior Rokach

A Survey of Data Leakage Detection and Prevention Solutions

Springer

Asaf Shabtai
Department of Information Systems
Engineering
Ben-Gurion University
Beer-Sheva, Israel

Lior Rokach
Department of Information Systems
Engineering
Ben-Gurion University
Beer-Sheva, Israel

Yuval Elovici
Department of Information Systems
Engineering
Telekom Innovation Laboratories
Ben-Gurion University
Beer-Sheva, Israel

ISSN 2191-5768   ISSN 2191-5776 (electronic)
ISBN 978-1-4614-2052-1 ISBN 978-1-4614-2053-8 (eBook)
DOI 10.1007/978-1-4614-2053-8
Springer New York Heidelberg Dordrecht London

Library of Congress Control Number: 2012932272

Printed on acid-free paper

Springer is part of Springer Science+Business Media (www.springer.com)

Preface

Information and data leakage pose a serious threat to companies and organizations as the number of leakage incidents and the cost they inflict continues to increase. Whether caused by malicious intent or by an inadvertent mistake, data loss can diminish a company's brand, reduce shareholder value, and damage the company's goodwill and reputation. Data leakage prevention (DLP) has been studied both in academic research areas and in practical application domains. This book aims to provide a structural and comprehensive overview of current research and practical solutions in the DLP domain. Existing solutions have been grouped into different categories based on a taxonomy described in the book. The taxonomy presented characterizes DLP solutions according to various aspects such as leakage source, data state, leakage channel, deployment scheme, prevention and detection approaches, and action taken upon leakage. In the commercial section solutions offered by the leading DLP market players are reviewed based on professional research reports and material obtained from vendor Web sites. In the academic section available academic studies have been clustered into various categories according to the nature of the leakage and the protection provided. Next, the main data leakage scenarios are described, each with the most relevant and applicable solution or approach that will mitigate and reduce the likelihood or impact of data leakage. In addition, several case studies of data leakage and data misuse are presented. Finally, the related research areas of privacy, data anonymization, and secure data publishing are discussed.

We would like to express our gratitude for all colleagues and graduate students that generously gave comments on drafts or counsel otherwise. We would like to express our special thanks to Jennifer Evans, Jennifer Maurer, Courtney Clark, and the staff members of Springer for their kind cooperation throughout the production of this book. We would like to thank to Prof. Zdonik, S., Prof. Ning, P., Prof. Shekhar, S., Prof. Katz, J., Prof. Wu, X., Prof. Jain, L.C., Prof. Padua, D., Prof. Shen, X., Prof. Furht, B. and Prof. Subrahmanian, V. for including our book in their important series (SpringerBriefs in Computer Science).

Beer-Sheva, Israel   Asaf Shabtai
                                                                                   Yuval Elovici
                                                                                   Lior Rokach

Contents

Chapter 1
Introduction to Information Security

The NIST Computer Security Handbook [NIST, 1995] defines the term *computer security* as "protection afforded to an automated information system in order to attain the applicable objectives of preserving the integrity, availability, and confidentiality of information system resources (includes hardware, software, firmware, information/data, and telecommunications)." The security concepts of confidentiality, integrity and availability are also called the CIA triad.

Confidentiality of information is typically seen as assurance that sensitive information is accessed only by authorized users. This task can be achieved by various mechanisms such as encryption and access control.

Integrity of information is typically seen as assurance that information is not modified by unauthorized users in a way that authorized users will not be able to identify the modification. This task can be achieved by various mechanisms such as digital signatures and message authentication code.

Availability is the task of ensuring that a system provides its services to its users at any point in time. Usually a system includes many mechanisms to ensure its availability, such as use of several independent power sources and multiple communication lines.

Nonrepudiation, access control, authentication, and privacy are concepts that are considered part of computer security as well.

Nonrepudiation ensures that a user who sends a message cannot deny that she is the originator of the message and furthermore, that the receiver of the message can prove in a court of law that she received the message from the sender.

Access control is the task of controlling which information and services a user may access after being identified. An access control mechanism can be used only if the user has been initially identified by the system. In many systems, every authorized action of the user is recorded by an *audit* mechanism.

Authentication is the task of verifying the identity of users who connect to a computerized system. This task can be achieved by the user's providing a unique secret

A. Shabtai et al., *A Survey of Data Leakage Detection and Prevention Solutions*,
SpringerBriefs in Computer Science, DOI 10.1007/978-1-4614-2053-8_1,
© The Author(s) 2012

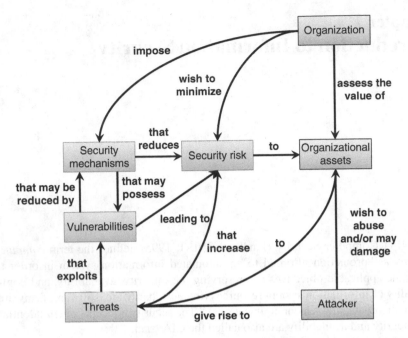

Fig. 1.1 Relationship among security terminology players (adapted from Stallings and Brown (2007))

such as a password (the user proves "what she knows"), using a unique token that the user possesses (the user proves "what she has"), or using some kind of biometric identification mechanism such as fingerprint (the user proves "what she is").

• *Privacy* relates to the task of certifying that a user has control of information collected about her and exposed to others. It is difficult to define the specific mechanisms used to ensure such user privacy. The entire system must be designed so that the user's privacy will not be violated.

Ensuring computer security is an extremely challenging task [Elovici, 2012]. In many cases, the security requirements are clear; however, it is less clear how to use the various mechanisms to meet these requirements. The security mechanism in many cases may become the next sensitive part of the system. For example, forcing the user to use a complex password may result in the user's writing a note with the password attached to the computer screen. Computer security is a continuous battle between the attackers who identify new security holes and vulnerabilities in systems and the organization's security department who must prevent them.

This book uses the security terminology proposed in [Stallings, 2007], which is presented in Figure 1.1. It is described here in the context of data leakage and data misuse.

The security terminology described in Figure 1.1 includes three physical players (organization, attackers, and organizational assets) and four logical players (security mechanisms, vulnerabilities, threats and security risks). The *organization* assesses the value of each of its organizational assets (database, server, etc.) In this book, the assets are mainly data and information which are stored in files or databases. The *organization* tries to minimize the *security risks* by putting the appropriate *security mechanisms* in place (firewall, intrusion prevention system, etc.) This book will focus mainly on security mechanisms that are related to information leakage detection and prevention. The *attackers* try to create *security threats* to compromise the *organization's assets*. In this book, the main goal of the attackers is to leak or misuse confidential information. The *organizational assets* are exposed to *security threats*. On the one hand, *security mechanisms* reduce existing *vulnerabilities*, yet on the other hand may create additional *vulnerabilities*. The *organization* also creates *vulnerabilities*, for instance, by not complying with its security policy. For example, in the context of this book, a user who provides his or her credentials to an unauthorized person makes the system vulnerable to attacks. *Vulnerabilities* are exploited by the *attackers*, in turn leading to risks to the *organizational assets*. In the context of this book, vulnerabilities will be used by the attacker in order to leak or misuse confidential information.

The following *computer and network security incident* taxonomy that is widely accepted by the computer and network security community describes all key players involved in security attack incidents. Each taxonomy description is accompanied by examples which relate to the topic of the book. The different parts of the taxonomy are:

- **Attacker**: an adversary that attempts to attack a computer, communication network, or both to fulfill an objective. In the data leakage context, the attacker may be an internal employee or an external attacker attempting to leak sensitive information.
- **Tool**: the means and methods that are used to perform the attack by exploiting the vulnerability in a computer, communication network or both, including *physical attack* (for example, physically accessing a computer and copying data) or *running a script or a malicious application* (for example, a Trojan horse uploading sensitive information to a remote server).
- **Vulnerability**: a weakness or flaw in the design, implementation or configuration of a system, communication network, or business process that in many cases is known only to the attackers. A common example is a super user such as the database administrator (DBA) or system administrator, who usually has full access to systems and data.
- **Action**: an act taken by the attackers to perform the attack and achieve the objective. For example, an action can be stealing user name and password using social engineering.
- **Target**: the component of the computer, communication network, or both that is the aim of the attack and usually includes a vulnerability. In the context of this book a target can be a server with confidential information.

- **Unauthorized result**: an unauthorized consequence of an event that will eventually lead to information leakage, data misuse or both.
- **Objectives**: the results expected by the attacker. In this book, the objective is either to leak or misuse confidential information.

Data leakage and data misuse are considered an emerging security threats to organizations, especially when carried out by insiders. In many cases, it is very difficult to detect insiders because they misuse their credentials to perform an attack. How can a security mechanism detect an insider who leaks confidential information to which she is exposed during her regular tasks in the organization? The vulnerabilities of internal systems are known to the insider and, in some cases, she might know which security mechanisms are used.

This book aims to provide a structural and comprehensive overview of current research and practical solutions in the DLP domain. Existing solutions have been grouped into different categories based on a taxonomy described in the book. The taxonomy presented characterizes DLP solutions according to various aspects such as leakage source, data state, leakage channel, deployment scheme, prevention and detection approaches, and action taken upon leakage.

Chapter 2
Data Leakage

Data leakage is defined as the *accidental or unintentional distribution of private or sensitive data to an unauthorized entity*. Sensitive data in companies and organizations include intellectual property (IP), financial information, patient information, personal credit-card data, and other information depending on the business and the industry. Data leakage poses a serious issue for companies as the number of incidents and the cost to those experiencing them continue to increase. Data leakage is enhanced by the fact that transmitted data (both inbound and outbound), including emails, instant messaging, website forms, and file transfers among others, are largely unregulated and unmonitored on their way to their destinations. Furthermore, in many cases, sensitive data are shared among various stakeholders such as employees working from outside the organization's premises (e.g., on laptops), business partners, and customers. This increases the risk that confidential information will fall into unauthorized hands. Whether caused by malicious intent or an inadvertent mistake by an insider or outsider, exposure of sensitive information can seriously hurt an organization. The potential damage and adverse consequences of a data leakage incident can be classified into two categories: direct and indirect losses. Direct losses refer to tangible damage that is easy to measure or to estimate quantitatively. Indirect losses, on the other hand, are much harder to quantify and have a much broader impact in terms of cost, place, and time [Bunker, 2009]. Direct losses include violations of regulations (such as those protecting customer privacy) resulting in fines, settlements or customer compensation fees; litigation involving lawsuits; loss of future sales; costs of investigation and remedial or restoration fees. Indirect losses include reduced share price as a result of negative publicity; damage to a company's goodwill and reputation; customer abandonment; and exposure of intellectual property (business plans, code, financial reports, and meeting agendas) to competitors.

A. Shabtai et al., *A Survey of Data Leakage Detection and Prevention Solutions*, SpringerBriefs in Computer Science, DOI 10.1007/978-1-4614-2053-8_2,
© The Author(s) 2012

Data leakage can occur in many forms and in any place. In a 2009 Data Breach Investigation Report[1] (by the Verizon Business RISK team), 90 data breaches occurring in 2008 were analyzed. In addition to the significant number of compromised records (285 million), the investigation revealed other interesting aspects of this problem as well. One of the most intriguing aspects revealed by the compiled data is that most breaches have been caused by external parties (74%). However, the number of breaches resulting exclusively from the actions of insiders is still significant (20%). Incidents in which business partners have been involved account for 32% of the total. According to the nonprofit consumer organization Privacy Rights Clearinghouse,[2] a total of 227,052,199 individual records containing sensitive personal information were involved in security breaches in the United States between January 2005 and May 2008.

Some recent high-profile leakage incidents, selected from www.datalossdb.org, are presented in Table 2.1. This sample of recent leakage incidents emphasizes the difficulty of providing a "one-stop-shop" silver-bullet solution for preventing all data leakage scenarios. The sample also indicates that enterprises should broaden the focus of their security efforts beyond merely securing network perimeters and internal hosts from classic threats (i.e., viruses, Trojan horses, worms, D/DoS attacks and intrusions). In addition, organizations are obligated to comply with federal and state regulations which aim to protecting financial and other private data by directing organizations to protect their networks and data. Examples of such regulations are the Health Insurance Portability and Accountability Act (HIPAA), the Gramm-Leach-Bliley Act (GLBA), California's data-breach disclosure notification law SB 1386, the Payment Card Industry Data Security Standard (PCI-DSS) and the Sarbanes–Oxley Act (SOX) [Frost & Sullivan, 2008].

In fact, according to the Gartner report [Ouellet, 2009], large enterprises already understand the need to use data leakage prevention (DLP) technology as one component in a comprehensive plan for the handling and transmission of sensitive data [Ouellet, 2009]. The technological means employed for enhancing DLP can be divided into the following categories (Figure 2.1): standard security measures, advanced/intelligent security measures, access control and encryption, and designated DLP systems [Phua, 2009].

Standard security measures are used by many organizations and include common mechanisms such as firewalls, intrusion detection systems (IDSs), and antivirus software that can provide protection against both outsider attacks (e.g., a firewall which limits access to the internal network and an intrusion detection system which detects attempted intrusions) and inside attacks (e.g., antivirus scans to detect a Trojan horse that may be installed on a PC to send confidential information). Another example is the use of thin clients which operate in a client-server architecture, with no personal or sensitive data stored on a client's computer. Policies and training for improving the awareness of employees and partners provide additional standard security measures.

---

[1] http://www.verizonbusiness.com/resources/security/reports/2009_databreach_rp.pdf
[2] http://www.privacyrights.org/ar/ChronDataBreaches.htm

Table 2.1 Data leakage incidents

Date	Organization	Description
Oct. 2008	UPS	A UPS employee's laptop containing payroll information for 9000 U.K. employees was stolen. In response UPS announced that it will encrypt all data stored on all the company's mobile devices.
Sept. 2011	Science Applications International Corp	Backup tapes stolen from a car containing 5,117,799 patients' names, phone numbers, Social Security numbers, and medical information.
Oct. 2009	U.S. National Archive	U.S. National Archive and Records administration improperly disposed of hard drives containing 76 million names, addresses, and SSNs of US military veterans.
July 2008	Google	Data were stolen, not from Google offices, but from the headquarters of an HR outsourcing company, Colt Express. The thieves broke in and stole company computers containing unencrypted data including names, addresses and SSNs of Google employees. As a result, Google terminated its partnership with Colt Express.
Jan. 2008	Stockport Primary Care Trust (U.K.)	A member of staff lost a USB memory stick containing data extracted from the medical records of patients. The data were being carried personally to avoid sending them by e-mail because the employee thought that they would be more secure.
June 2004	AOL	An employee of America Online Inc. stole the computerized employee identification code of another AOL worker to gain access to AOL's subscriber data. He then stole 92 million email addresses belonging to 30 million subscribers and sold them to spammers.
July 2009	American Express	DBA stole a laptop containing thousands of American Express card numbers. The DBA reported it stolen, "...he (DBA) was one of the few who could have possibly downloaded all their account holders' information, including the PIN numbers used to access money from ATM machines at various banks."
2007	Wagner Resource Group	An employee of a McLean investment firm decided to trade some music using a file-sharing network while using the company computer. In doing so, he inadvertently opened the private files of his firm, Wagner Resource Group, to the public. Social Security numbers, dates of birth, and names of 2,000 clients were exposed.
Aug. 2007	Nuclear Laboratory in Los Alamos	An employee of the U.S. nuclear laboratory in Los Alamos transmitted confidential information by email. The incident was classified as a serious threat to the country's nuclear safety.

(continued)

Table 2.1 (continued)

Date	Organization	Description
Feb. 2008	Eli Lilly & Co.	One of Eli Lilly & Co.'s subcontracted lawyers at Philadelphia-based Pepper Hamilton mistakenly emailed confidential Eli Lilly discussions to *Times* reporter Alex Berenson (instead of to Bradford Berenson, her co-counsel), costing Eli Lilly nearly $1 billion.
Sep. 2007	Scarborough & Tweed	The Web servers of Scarborough & Tweed, a company that sells corporate gifts online, were compromised and information about 570 customers may have been accessed using an SQL injection attack. The information included customers' names, addresses, telephone numbers, account numbers, and credit card numbers.
May 2009	Alberta Health Services	Personal health information on thousands of Albertans was skimmed from the Alberta Health Services Edmonton network as a computer virus infected the network and stole medical information on 1,582 people, including laboratory test results and diagnostic imaging reports. The virus captured information from a computer screen and then transmitted it to an external website.
Apr. 2009	Prague hotel (Czech Republic)	A data leakage incident occurred in a Prague hotel (Czech Republic). The flight details and passport numbers of approximately 200 EU leaders were leaked by accident. The data was related to an EU-US summit held in Prague and attended by U.S. President Obama.
Jan. 2009	Heartland Payment Systems	Malicious software/hack compromised tens of millions of credit and debit card transactions. "The data include the digital information encoded onto the magnetic stripe … thieves can fashion counterfeit credit cards…"
2003	British Intelligence	A British intelligence report in the form of a Word document containing the names of the authors of a paper in its revision log metadata was cited by the United States in a speech to the United Nations. The metadata showed that the report was in fact written by U.S. researchers.

Creating and enforcing organization-wide data handling policies based on industry regulations and on the organization's specific requirements is essential to regulate all aspects of handling personal data in an organization. These policies declare strict rules for handling these data, such as discarding or archiving unneeded personal data and creating access control mechanisms to enable access to such data by authorized employees only. The creation of a data handling policy should be accompanied by appropriate training that informs employees of the rules and a requirement

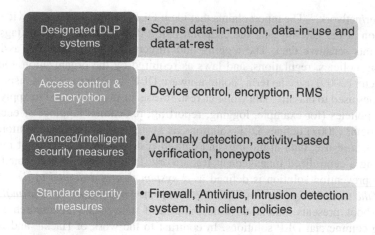

Fig. 2.1 Categories of technological approaches used to provide data leakage detection and prevention

that employees sign binding statements regarding their responsibilities and their commitment to work according to the policy.

Advanced or intelligent security measures include machine learning and temporal reasoning algorithms for detecting abnormal access to data (i.e., databases or information retrieval systems), activity-based verification (e.g., based on keystrokes and mouse patterns), detection of abnormal email exchange patterns, and applying the honeypot concept for detecting malicious insiders.

Device control, access control, and encryption are used to prevent access by an unauthorized user. These are the simplest measures that can be taken to protect large amounts of personal data against malicious outsider and insider attacks.

Designated DLP solutions are intended to detect and prevent attempts to copy or send sensitive data, intentionally or unintentionally, without authorization, mainly by personnel who are authorized to access the sensitive information. A major capability of such solutions is an ability to classify content as sensitive. Designated DLP solutions are typically implemented using mechanisms such as exact data matching, structured data fingerprinting, statistical methods (e.g., machine learning), rule and regular expression matching, published lexicons, conceptual definitions and keywords [Ouellet, 2009].

This survey focuses mainly on the category of designated Data Leakage Prevention (DLP) solutions, often referred to as *Information Leak Prevention* (ILP), *Data Leak/Loss Prevention* (DLP), *Outbound Content Compliance, Content Monitoring and Filtering, Content Monitoring and Protection* (CMP), or *Extrusion Prevention* [Mogull, 2007].

Several definitions have been proposed for describing designated DLP solutions. Frost & Sullivan (2008) defined a DLP solution as a "system that monitors and enforces policies on fingerprinted data that are at-rest (i.e., in storage), in-motion (i.e., across a network) or in-use (i.e., during an operation) on a public or private computer/network. " The report claims that ideal DLP solutions should provide data protection at the gateway and the endpoint using data discovery, which tags and fingerprints sensitive data. The tagging and fingerprinting of data will assist in enforcing policies, regulations, and laws as required by the organization. Ouellet and Proctor (2009) uses the term "content-aware DLP" to refer to a set of inspection techniques used to classify data while at-rest, in-use, or in-motion and to apply pre-defined policies (for example, logging, reporting, relocating, tagging, or encrypt-ing). Mogull (2007) defines DLP solutions as systems that identify, monitor, and protect data-in-use, data-in-motion, and data-at-rest through deep content inspec-tion using a centralized management framework. In this work, a designated data leakage prevention solution is defined as *a system that is designed to detect and prevent the unauthorized access, use, or transmission of confidential information.*

This book presents a methodical description of state-of-the-art research and of existing commercial DLP solutions. In contrast to the work of Hackle and Hauer (2009) who have focused on the domain of commercial DLP products, here both commercial solutions and academic research will be discussed and analyzed. To the best of the authors' knowledge, this survey is the first to provide a review and discus-sion of both research and existing commercial DLP solutions. A taxonomy of DLP solutions and a classification of the security measures used for DLP will first be presented. Second, the main data leakage scenarios will be described, with for each scenario, the most relevant and applicable solution or approach that will mitigate and reduce the likelihood and impact of the leakage scenario.

Chapter 3
A Taxonomy of Data Leakage Prevention Solutions

DLP solutions can be characterized according to a taxonomy that incorporates the following attributes: data state, deployment scheme, leakage handling approach, and action taken upon leakage (Figure 3.1).

3.1 What to protect? (data-state)

DLP solutions distinguish between three phases of data throughout their lifecycle: data-at-rest (DAR), data-in-motion (DIM) and data-in-use (DIU).

Data-At-Rest are defined as all data in computer storage. To keep data-at-rest from being accessed, stolen, or altered by unauthorized people, security measures such as data encryption and access control are commonly used. A prerequisite for these security measures is content discovery, which serves to find where all the data are stored. One way to achieve this is using the content discovery features of DLP products. For example, a policy may require that customer credit card numbers be stored only on approved servers. If data are detected on an unauthorized server, they can be encrypted or removed, or a warning can be sent to the data owner.

Data-In-Use are any data with which a user is interacting. Endpoint-related systems are used to protect data-in-use and to monitor data as the user interacts with them. Usually, an agent is used to monitor the data while they are being used or transported from an endpoint device or client through different output channels to peripheral devices. The underlying idea is that if an attempt is made to send sensitive data, the potential leakage will be immediately detected and tackled (e.g., blocked) before the data can be sent. Data-in-use tools may monitor the following activities:

- Copy-and-paste and screen-capture operations involving sensitive data.
- Transfer of sensitive content from one place to another using portable storage device such as USB drives, CD/DVDs, smartphones, and PDAs.
- Printing or faxing sensitive content.

A. Shabtai et al., *A Survey of Data Leakage Detection and Prevention Solutions*,
SpringerBriefs in Computer Science, DOI 10.1007/978-1-4614-2053-8_3,
© The Author(s) 2012

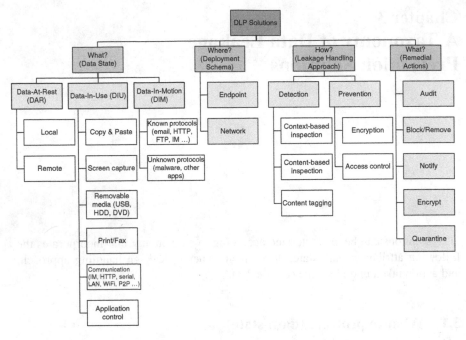

Fig. 3.1 A taxonomy of data leakage prevention (DLP) solutions

- Attempts to transmit sensitive content through communication channels. For example, deliberately or unintentionally posting sensitive data in the form of typed content, attached files or voice conversations through an IM application or a Web site, or copying sensitive content to a shared folder in a LAN.
- Use of sensitive data in an unapproved application (such as trying to encrypt data for the purpose of sneaking it past the sensors).

Data-In-Motion are data that are being sent through a network. These data may be sent inside the internal network of an organization or may cross over into an external network. DLP solutions are used to detect and inspect data which are being sent across communication channels over a network using known protocols, including email, http, instant messaging, and even unknown protocols (by simply inspecting the packets' content). If encryption or encrypted connections are permitted without the ability to decrypt the data, a DLP solution will not be able to detect leakage of encrypted sensitive data-in-motion.

3.2   Where to protect? (deployment scheme)

Two main deployment options are used when installing DLP products:

Endpoint: DLP software deployed directly on endpoint devices or clients. This software monitors and controls access to data while a remote supervisory server takes in charge of administrative duties, policy distribution and generation of log events. Agents need to operate within the resource constraints of the endpoint while providing an acceptable level of protection. They typically protect data as they are being used by the user (data-in-use) and detect sensitive data stored on the endpoint (data-at-rest). An endpoint agent can protect systems even when they are disconnected from the network.

Network: A DLP solution can be deployed on the network level. By analyzing network traffic, and subject to a predefined policy, events can be fired and suspicious transmissions blocked. A network-based DLP system should be able to support multiple monitoring points in the network, while a central management server collects and analyzes the data obtained from all monitoring points.

3.3   How to protect? (leakage handling approach)

Leakage incidents can be handled using two main approaches: detective approaches and preventive approaches.

In a *detective approach*, the system will attempt to detect leakage incidents and will take the proper corrective action to handle any identified leakage incident. For example, when a local DLP agent detects a file containing sensitive information on an un-authorized server, it can move the file to a safe location, such as a secured repository. Context-based inspection, content-based inspection, and content tagging are forms of detection approaches.

Context-based inspection leverages the abundant security technologies such as firewalls, proxies, intrusion detection/prevention systems (IDS/IPS), and spam filtering. The term *context* refers to contextual information extracted from the monitored data, such as source, destination, size, recipients, sender, header/metadata information, time stamps, file type, location, format, application, and queries or transactions. An example of a context inspection-based system is the packet-filter firewall, which decides whether a network packet will be allowed to pass through on the basis of explicit filtering criteria such as source/destination IP address, source/destination port, and other packet attributes. A context-based DLP solution can prevent Java files from being sent out of an organization, block all encrypted files, or prevent copy-and-paste operations from specific applications.

Content-based inspection: this approach detects data leakage by analyzing content using a variety of techniques such as:

- A combination of lexicons containing keywords such as "confidential," "financial report," "project XYZ," and patterns or regular expression matching (e.g., a 16-digit pattern for a credit card number). Most products come with common dictionaries that address regulations and laws such as PCI-DSS, HIPAA, GLBA, and SOX. This type of detection technique is the easiest and fastest to configure, but provides little protection in the case of unstructured data.

- Fingerprinting: a method that extracts "fingerprints" from sensitive files or database entries and searches for exact fingerprints to detect leakage. A *fingerprint* is a preferably unique hash value associate with a set of data. Hash values for all sensitive files are stored in databases or locally on the machine under inspection. The system compares these hash values with portions of the inspected data. Fingerprints can be created on database records (e.g., CCNs that actually appear in the database).
- Natural-language analysis: detects whether sensitive data and inspected data are similar using natural language analysis. The technical details of such methods are usually not revealed by the solution providers.
- Statistics: this approach involves extracting statistical metrics obtained from the content under inspection (e.g., frequency of terms) and using machine learning methods similar to those used for blocking spam. This method is efficient for detecting unstructured content in cases where a deterministic technique is difficult to implement and statistical metrics are the best approach available.
- Although it is not difficult to look inside plain text such as an email message, problems arise when dealing with content that is not plain text, such as binary files. A DLP solution should provide "file-cracking" capabilities to interpret a file when the content is obscured several levels down; for example, when an Excel spreadsheet is embedded in a zipped Word file.

Content tagging: in this approach, a tag is assigned to a file containing sensitive data, and a policy is enforced based on the assigned tag. Content will remain tagged even when processed by other applications. For example, a Word document file that was tagged as sensitive will remain tagged as sensitive even when it is encrypted or zipped. Tags can be assigned to files in different ways: manually by the creator of the sensitive data; automatically using content- or context-based analysis; automatically to all files stored in a specified location; or automatically to all files created by specific applications or users.

In a *preventive approach*, potential leakage incidents are prevented before they occur by taking proper measures. DLP solutions support prevention of data leakage using several preventive approaches:

Access control: this approach provides the ability to permit or deny the use of a particular resource by a particular entity. DLP can restrict the use of information, as determined by the policy, if access to sensitive information has been granted. One way to achieve access control is by integration with enterprise digital rights management (EDRM) to apply access control to documents automatically.

Disabling functions: this preventative approach involves disabling functionalities that can result in inappropriate use of sensitive data. This can be done, for example, by restricting copy-and-paste operations on sensitive content, by restricting the copying of content to portable storage, or by implementing thin clients.

Encryption: defines a policy which states what sensitive data must be encrypted and who is allowed to request decryption of these data. It also restricts applications which are allowed to use sensitive data by allowing encryption only with an approved enterprise solution.

Awareness: involves raising the consciousness level of employees by informing them of who has access to what, which data are particularly sensitive, and what needs to be done to ensure that data are not misused.

Chapter 4
Data Leakage Detection/Prevention Solutions

4.1 A review of commercial DLP solutions

4.1.1 Market overview

According to the Forrester Wave report [Raschke, 2008], most early DLP solutions focused on finding sensitive data as they left the organizational network by monitoring data-in-motion at the various network egress points. In the second stage, as removable storage devices (e.g., USB sticks, external hard drives) proliferated, DLP solutions began to focus on detecting data leakage at the endpoint and on providing capabilities, for example, to subvert copying of sensitive information to USB devices or CD/DVDs even if the endpoint is not connected to the network.

The biggest DLP challenge lies in protecting the large amounts of sensitive data which exist in unstructured form (e.g., various types of intellectual property like source code, customer lists, and product designs). Therefore, DLP solution providers are continuously improving their data discovery methods using approaches such as fingerprinting and natural-language processing [Frost & Sullivan, 2008].

According to three leading research reports, in the next few years, DLP products are expected to become as stable and as commonplace as existing security solutions such as firewalls, intrusion detection systems and anti-malware solutions [Frost & Sullivan, 2008], [Raschke, 2008], [Ouellet, 2009].

4.1.2 Technological offerings of market leaders

Based on the taxonomy described in Chapter 3, the main DLP functionalities offered by the market leaders will now be described. A representative example of a DLP system architecture (from TrendMicro systems) has been presented by Lawton (2008). These functionalities will be characterized based on the state of the data which they aim to protect (i.e., in-use, at-rest, or in-motion).

A. Shabtai et al., *A Survey of Data Leakage Detection and Prevention Solutions*,
SpringerBriefs in Computer Science, DOI 10.1007/978-1-4614-2053-8_4,
© The Author(s) 2012

Protection for data-at-rest is provided by content discovery solutions that scan workstations and laptops, mass storage (e.g., file servers), email servers, document management systems, and databases in an attempt to detect sensitive data stored in unauthorized locations. There are two basic techniques for content discovery:

- *Local scanning (i.e., agent-based)*: In this technique, an agent is installed on a machine and locally scans for content stored on a host that violates a policy. If such data are found, common actions include relocation, encryption and quarantine. Although this technique has the disadvantage that agents are limited by their processing power and memory on the target system (because they use local CPU cycles), its main advantage is that it can always be active and enforcing the policy even if the local device is not connected to the network.
- *Remote scanning*: Scanning is performed remotely by making a connection to a server or device using a file-sharing or application protocol. The disadvantage of this technique is that it increases network traffic and has performance limitations based on available network bandwidth and the constraints of the target machine.

Protection for data-at-rest is also provided by encryption of data at the endpoint. This can be done using full-disk encryption or file-level encryption with access control. Encryption will protect sensitive data if, for example, a laptop is stolen or lost.

Protection for data-in-use is provided by a local, host-based agent that locally monitors and prevents actions involving sensitive data, such as copy-and-paste, print-screen, copying to a USB/CD/DVD, unauthorized data transmission, or use of data in unapproved applications.

Protection for data-in-motion is provided by means of a network-based solution that searches for and blocks content that violates a policy. Network monitoring components are often deployed at or near the enterprise gateway. They perform full-packet capture, session reconstruction, and content analysis in real time. Usually, a proxy provides deep content inspection across various protocols (primarily HTTP, FTP, and IM). Email integration (i.e., embedding of a mail transport agent (MTA)) is typically used to inspect email and to enable quarantine, encryption, or filtering of suspicious emails.

An important feature provided by most DLP products is a centralized administrative system that enables specification of sensitive data (e.g., a regular expression that matches a credit card number) and rules that specify which actions should be taken when sensitive data leakage is detected. Rules can be user-specific (i.e., applied only to a specific user or groups of users), can specify what type of data to check (e.g., only email messages and web forms, or only data stored in MS SharePoint), and can define cardinality (e.g., more than 5 CCNs in the same email) and proximity (e.g., Name and ID in the same email are OK; but Name, ID, and medical data are not OK). Examples of such rules are:

(1) An email detected as containing sensitive data based on fingerprint comparison should be redirected to the encryption gateway.

(2) A file containing the "project XYZ" keyword should have the MS-Rights Management System applied to restrict access to the file.
(3) A file containing SSNs in publicly accessed locations should be relocated to the secure server T.

The administrative system also makes it possible to propagate policy updates throughout the DLP system modules, to browse reports and alerts regarding policy violations, and to investigate and handle leakage incidents. Therefore, an important feature of the administrative system is the capability to replay leakage incidents with all relevant data about user actions (such as keystrokes, files opened, and Web sites visited) preceding or following a leakage incident.

Table 4.1 summarizes the main products available and the functionalities they provide according to the taxonomy presented in Chapter 3.

4.1.3   Conclusions, remarks, and problems with the state of the art in industrial DLP

From analysis of the DLP market, it is evident that designated DLP technology is relatively young and that its market structure is therefore characterized by large security vendors that have acquired small DLP solution providers specializing in specific data leakage scenarios.

The importance of DLP solutions is well understood by DLP solution providers and other related security vendors, and therefore there has been a trend to bundle DLP features into standard security technologies in an effort to provide holistic protection of sensitive data. Examples of this trend include integration with rights management systems (e.g., McAfee with Adobe RMS; RSA with MS-RMS), integration with MS Sharepoint (e.g., RSA), integration with Web-filtering capabilities (e.g., Websense) and integration with virtualization frameworks (e.g., RSA integration with VMWare). However, DLP solutions typically provide little or no defense against intra-organizational data leakage (between departments), but focus rather on preventing leaks beyond the organization's perimeter. Integration with virtualization frameworks should enable organizations to provide internal DLP with low effort.

The most important task when deploying a DLP product is defining the initial policy and providing the sensitive content that will be used by the system to extract its representation of sensitive content. In most cases, the organization is required to provide a set of sensitive documents in order to set up the system. This is not a trivial task, especially for large organizations. Adding new, organization-specific rules is also a difficult task because the false positive rate of the detection engine must be taken into consideration.

Table 4.1 DLP commercial products offering[1]

	Symantec	Websense	McAfee	Verdasys	RSA	Vericept	Raytheon-Oakley	Safend	Sophos	Fidelis	Trend-Micro	GTB
What? (data state)												
Data-At-Rest												
Local	+	+	+	+	+	+	+	+	−	−	+	−
Remote	+	+	+	+	+	+	−	−	−	−	−	+
Data-In-Use												
Copy & Paste	+	+	+	+	+	+	+	+	+	+	+	+
Screen capture	+	+	+	+	+	−	+	−	+	−	−	?
Removable media	+	+	+	+	+	+	+	+	+	+	+	+
Print, fax	+	+	+	+	+	+	+	+	+	+	+	+
Communication	+	+	+	+	+	+	+	+	+	+	+	+
Application control	+	+	+	−	+	−	+	+	−	+	−	+
Data-In-Motion												
Known protocols	+	+	+	+	+	+	+	+	+	+	+	+
Unknown protocols	+	−	+	−	+	+	?	+	−	+	−	+
Where? (deployment)												
Endpoint	+	+	+	+	+	−	+	+	+	+	+	+
Network	+	+	+	+	+	+	+	+	−	+	+	+
How? (leakage handling approach)												
Detection												
Context-based	+	+	+	+	+	−	+	−	+	+	+	+
Content-based	+	+	+	+	+	+	+	+	+	+	+	+
Content tagging	−	−	−	−	−	−	−	−	−	−	−	−
Prevention												
Encryption	−	−	−	−	−	−	−	−	−	−	−	−
Access control	−	−	−	−	−	−	−	−	−	−	−	−
Disabling function	−	−	−	−	−	−	−	−	−	−	−	−
What? (remedial action)												
Audit	+	+	+	+	+	+	+	+	+	+	+	+
Block/Remove	+	+	+	+	+	+	+	+	+	+	+	+
Notify	+	+	+	+	+	+	+	+	+	+	+	+
Encrypt	+	+	+	+	+	+	−	+	−	−	+	+
Quarantine	+	+	−	+	+	+	−	−	−	−	−	+

[1]Note that this table was derived using professional research reports and material obtained from vendors Web sites. Features that could not be determined were marked with "?"

Currently, DLP solutions do not include an inherent alert-correlation capability, that is, with other alerts raised by the same DLP system or by other security systems (e.g., IDS, anti-malware). For example, the fact that user u attempted to email file f outside the organization (and was blocked) has no correlation with the same user printing the same file one minute later (which is allowed) or encrypting the same file. This makes it hard to analyze the reports provided by such systems, especially in large organizations with hundreds of incidents per day.

Finally, from analysis of the detection methods used by these products, the authors have concluded that designated DLP solutions are prescribed mainly for mitigating accidental leakage incidents. This conclusion is supported by the fact that the detection methods used by most solution providers are very simple and limited and can easily be bypassed by replacing keywords and phrases in structured data to evade detection by regular expressions and other common mechanisms. Fingerprinting can also be bypassed with minimal effort by replacing a single word or character to yield a false negative. Moreover, during the fingerprinting process, care should be taken to make sure that insensitive text is not fingerprinted as well. Mitigation of intentional data leakage incidents is provided mainly by incorporating disk and file encryption, DRM services or both.

4.2   Academic research in the DLP domain

In recent years, the challenge of dealing with the malicious insider has been acknowledged, and several methods have been proposed for solving this problem. Data leakage is one of the main goals of a malicious insider [Salem, 2008], and therefore most of the methods proposed for insider threat detection are also applicable for detecting and preventing data leakage.

Initially, Maybury et al. (2005) presented the results of a collaborative study involving a characterization and analysis of the methods used to counter malicious insiders in the U.S. intelligence community. The study proposes a generic model of malicious insider behavior, distinguishing motives, actions, and associated observables. Several prototype techniques were developed for providing early warning of malicious insider activity, including the use of honeytokens, network traffic profiling, and knowledge-based algorithms for structured analysis and data fusion. The performance of these techniques was measured in an operational network against three distinct classes of insiders (an analyst, an application administrator, and a system administrator). Gaonjur and Bokhoree (2006) focused on the risks of insider threats in information technology (IT) outsourcing and proposed mitigation of these risks using non-deceptive techniques such as intrusion-detection systems and deceptive techniques such as honeypots. A properly secured network with appropriate intrusion-detection systems and honeypot configuration will ensure the overall security and integrity of users' sensitive information. Salem et al. (2008) and recently Hong et al. (2010) surveyed proposed methods for detecting insider attack in the research literature, including host-based user profiling based on features such as database and file system accesses, system calls, and OS commands; network-based detection; and use of honeypots. One example is the framework presented in [Bowen, 2009b] which combines host-based behavioral detection with modules that can create and monitor decoy (bait) documents [Bowen, 2009b]. The host-based sensor applies anomaly detection on data extracted from the system on registry as well as DLL activity, running processes, and GUI access [Salem, 2011a].

Franqueira et al. (2010) distinguished between internal insiders and external insiders (e.g., contractors and business partners). They surveyed various detection methods, including auditing, updating access rights, behavior monitoring, security policies and security assurance, and indicated the key differences when applying these methods for detecting internal and external insiders. The authors noted that external insiders are not subject to the same security measures that are used for detecting malicious internal insiders. Therefore, mitigating the external insider threat should start with evaluating the extent of the potential insider threat by mapping the data being shared, the business partners, etc. In addition, contracts specifying, for example, what each business partner (external insider) is allowed and not allowed to do with the data are essential.

The following sections present the academic literature related to data leakage detection and prevention (also summarized in Table 4.2). This literature can be clustered into the following categories:

1. **Misuse detection in information retrieval (IR) systems**. Focuses on detecting authorized users who use an IR system to retrieve and view documents that should not be viewed by that user.
2. **Misuse detection in databases**. Focuses on detecting anomalous patterns of database system access by authorized users.
3. **Email leakage protection**. Data mining technology has been successfully used to provide both signature-based misuse detection and anomaly detection-based misuse discovery automatically. The application of this technology can include either email content inspection or behavior-based analyses, such as detection of groups of user accounts that communicate with each other [Stolfo, 2006]. Both approaches can be meshed and interoperated to provide more strict enforcement.
4. **Network/Web-based protection**. As the Internet grows and network bandwidth continues to increase, organizations are faced with the task of keeping confidential information from leaving their networks. To handle the high volume of network traffic, researchers have attempted to create data-loss prevention systems that check outgoing traffic for known confidential information. These systems stop naïve adversaries from leaking data, but are fundamentally unable to identify encrypted or obfuscated information leaks [Borders, 2008].
5. **Encryption and access control**. Robust content protection requires ensuring that the environment where the content is accessed, stored and transferred is secure and protected. The main point in this scheme is to ensure that content can be accessed only by authorized devices and users [Abbadi, 2008].
6. **Data hidden in files**. Hiding sensitive information in a document is not sufficient because users can use common knowledge (e.g., "all patients in the same ward

Table 4.2 Summary of academic solutions

Reference	Category	Method
[Ma, 2005]	Information retrieval system	User profiling based on keywords in queries and search results (relevance feedback).
[Cathey, 2003]	Information retrieval system	User profiling based on query results and relevance feedback.
[Mun, 2008]	Information retrieval system	Assigning privilege levels to users and security level to documents and monitoring user access to documents.
[Kamra, 2008]	Database	Using machine learning methods to detect abnormal access behavior by analyzing query syntax.
[Sunu, 2009]	Database	Using machine learning methods to detect abnormal access behavior by analyzing query result-sets.
[Gafny, 2010] [Gafny, 2011]	Database	Using supervised and unsupervised learning to detect abnormal access behavior by analyzing query result-sets and contextual information.
[Harel, 2010] [Harel, 2011a] [Harel, 2011b] [Harel, 2012]	Database	Assigning a misusability score which estimates potential damage by measuring the sensitivity of the data that was exposed to the user.
MDAD[Fonseca, 2008]	Database	IDS - Learns a graph of user transactions by examining DBMS audit trail.
[Yaseen, 2009]	Database	Modeling the knowledge that an insider can infer from relational database systems.
[Carvalho, 2007] [Carvalho, 2009]	Email	Outlier-based detection of typical recipients along with textual content analysis.
[Stolfo, 2006]	Email	Outlier-based detection of typical recipients along with textual content analysis.
[Zilberman,2010] [Zlberman,2011]	Email	Analysis of the email exchange among groups of members of the organization to detect email leakage incidents.
Elicit system [Caputo, 2009]	Network/Web-based protection	Monitoring users' access to information on an intranet using network-based sensors which generate information-use events. These events are combined with contextual information and processed by various rule-based and statistical detectors that may issue alerts.
[Abbadi, 2008] [Alawneh, 2008]	Encryption and access control	Encryption and access control.
CLAMP [Parno, 2009]	Access control to database server	Access control isolation.
Web-based DLP [Yasuhiro, 2002]	Encryption and access control	Encryption and access control
[De Capitani, 2010]	Encryption and access control	Application of selective encryption to provide selective access control to outsourced sensitive data by third-party partners.
[Byers, 2004]	Data hidden in files	Awareness

(continued)

Table 4.2 (continued)

Reference	Category	Method
[Yixiang, 2007]	Infer sensitive data from published documents	"Eliminate Inner Nodes" algorithm serves to find a maximal partial document without causing information leakage when publishing several related XML documents, while allowing the publishing of as much data as possible.
DDD [Bowen, 2009a] [Salem, 2011b]	Honeytokens	Web-based service generates and distributes decoy documents to registered users and monitors any activity associated with the honeytokens planted into them.
[Čenys, 2005]	Honeytokens	Insertion of a honeytable into the database which is able to attract malicious users.
[Storey, 2009] [Spitzner, 2003]	Honeytokens	Planting of honeytokens into genuine system resources (e.g., network traffic).
[White, 2009] [White, 2010]	Honeytokens	Focuses on generating honeytokens.
[Papadimitriou, 2010]	Honeytokens; insider threat	Distributes sensitive data objects (including honeytokens) to several agents in such a way that the data owner will be able to identify the source of leakage with high probability.
[Berkovitch, 2011]	Honeytokens	Presents HoneyGen, a framework for generating honeytokens that appear real and that are difficult to distinguish from real tokens.
[Salem, 2011a] [Bowen, 2009b]	Insider threat	Methods for detecting malicious insiders including host-based user profiling based on features such as database and file system access patterns, system calls, and OS commands; network-based detection; and use of honeypots.

have the same disease") to infer more data, which can cause leakage of sensitive information [Yixiang, 2007]. The need to hide secret information in one or multiple documents is highly relevant for XML documents shared across business partners over the Web.

7. **Detecting malicious insiders using honeypots and honeytokens**. In this approach honeytokens or honeyfiles are planted in an organization's applications or machines (e.g., fake user IDs and passwords, or fake employees salary data). This information can then direct the insider to more advanced honeypots where actions can be monitored in an attempt to reveal true intentions.

4.2.1 Misuse detection in information retrieval (IR) systems

The typical approach proposed for detecting data leakage in information retrieval (IR) systems is anomaly detection. Generally, the system learns the normal behavioral profile of a user (or a group of users) and detects deviations or anomalies with reference to this profile. The key question in an anomaly detection approach is how to model users' behavior. Cathey et al. (2003) proposed four methods for modeling behavior in IR systems: document clustering, clustering query results, relevance feedback, and the fusion method.

Document clustering operates in three phases. First, all documents in the IR system are clustered based on their content. Next, during the training phase, the misuse detection system builds a user profile based on the clusters of documents retrieved by a user's queries. The assumption in this model is that a user who usually queries documents in a certain cluster should also be permitted to retrieve any other document in that same cluster. However, when a user attempts to access a document that belongs to a cluster which he or she does not normally access and when this cluster is not similar to any of the "normally accessed" clusters, an alarm is raised. Thus, during the detection phase, the detection system detects a retrieval misuse incident by comparing actually retrieved documents with a user's profile. The severity of a warning is based on the distance between the document and the nearest profile cluster.

Clustering query results is similar to document clustering, only in this method, the documents being clustered are only those previously accessed by the user (as opposed to all the documents in the IR system). The documents that the user has accessed in the past are usually only a small fraction of the full document dataset, meaning that fewer documents are clustered.

In the *relevance feedback* approach, the submitted query is analyzed, and keywords are identified (keysetQuery). In addition, the documents currently being accessed by a user are also analyzed, and keywords are extracted from them as well using standard relevance feedback algorithms (keysetFeedback). A user profile is defined as a combined set of keywords that a user has queried or accessed (keysetQuery ∪ keysetFeedback). When the user submits a new query, the query's keywords are extracted, and if the number of keywords that do not appear in the synthesized user profile exceeds some threshold, an alarm is fired.

Finally, the *fusion method* simply combines all previous methods in a weighted average to determine when to raise the alarm.

Experimental evaluations performed by Cathey et al. (2003) indicated that the relevance feedback and fusion methods provided the best overall results. A high degree of accuracy (92%) was also reported when taking the most significant 10% of alarms and reporting them as intrusions. Ma and Gohrian (2005) tested the relevance feedback method for a user who submits a short (up to four terms) or a long query (up to 17 terms). The results of this evaluation had an overall precision of 83.9% and 82.2% for short and long queries respectively. The rate of undetected misuse for short queries was less than 2% and for long queries less than 6%. Gohrian et al. (2005) extended the work of [Ma, 2005] and evaluated machine learning algorithms for automated adjustments of weights assigned to various components of the user profile and the user query in this detection process (the weights were previously adjusted manually). Four classifiers (SVM, ANN, BN, and C4.5) were compared with the manual adjustment approach as a baseline. Three scenarios were evaluated: short queries used for deriving profiles and for detection; long queries used for deriving profiles and for detection; and long queries used for deriving profiles and short queries used for detection. The results demonstrate that for each of the tested scenarios, one or more of the classifiers performs as well as or better than the manual adjustment.

Mun et al. (2008) proposed the use of an intrusion detection system for detecting insider attackers. The proposed system is based on assigning grades and privilege levels to users and security levels to documents and monitoring user access to documents.

4.2.2   Misuse detection in databases

Several related studies have dealt with detecting anomalous accesses to databases. The research reported sought to protect data in databases under several scenarios, for example an insider who is authorized to access the database (through management or other applications), but who submits anomalous queries that might indicate possible data misuse (e.g., data harvesting); an insider who abuses his or her legitimate privileges to masquerade as another user to gather data for malicious purposes; or an outside attacker who tries to extract data (e.g., using SQL injection).

Most of the proposed methods focus on learning the normal query patterns of users or roles and, during the monitoring phase, identifying abnormal queries. The studies differ in how the queries are represented.

Two main types of features are used to model a query: syntax-centric and data-centric. *The syntax-centric* approach relies on the SQL expression syntax of queries to construct user profiles. The *data-centric* approach focuses on what the user is trying to access instead of how he or she expresses the request. Consequently, in the data-centric approach, the query is modeled by extracting features from the query result set, such as the number of tuples and the minimum, maximum and average values of attributes.

Both approaches assume a mapping among users, queries, and query results. This is not the case with most Web-based applications which authenticate to databases with a different application user.

Kamra et al. (2008) evaluated a syntax-centric approach for detecting data misuse in database management systems (DBMS) which process SQL query logs to create profiles of the "normal" database access behavior of users. If each user is associated with a role, the system will learn the normal behavior pattern of each role, and deviations from these patterns will then be detected. Otherwise, users are clustered based on their behavior. Each cluster is then treated as a role to detect a user who behaves similarly to those of another cluster. An outlier detection algorithm identifies user behavior which deviates from the profiles.

Each query is represented by extracting features from the query syntax. The extracted features refer to SQL commands, accessed relational information, and accessed attribute information. The information can be extracted at three levels of granularity: coarse-grained (the least detailed; contains information such as number of distinct relations and attributes accessed in the command); medium-grained (contains more detail, such as counting the number of attributes accessed in each relation accessed by the query); and fine-grained (the most detailed, explicitly lists which attributes in which relation were accessed).

The evaluation of the proposed method was conducted using a naïve Bayes classifier and a real dataset consisting of 7,583 SELECT commands, 213 INSERT commands, and 572 UPDATE commands and anomalous queries that were generated and injected into the datasets. The results indicated a false negative rate of 2.4% and a false positive rate of 17.9% when using the fine-grained features.

The proposed method is simple to implement and to integrate with database systems. It is also lightweight because the structural features of a query can be extracted fairly quickly. However, the syntax-centric approach is error-prone. For example, it may result in two queries which differ widely in syntax and yet which produce the same "normal" or "abnormal" decision.

Sunu et al. (2009) proposed a method of statistically profiling normal user database access (query) patterns and indicating when a user deviates from his or her routine. The authors use the data-centric approach and consider the query expression syntax irrelevant for discriminating user intent; only the resulting data matter. According to the proposed approach, a statistical "summary" of the query's result tuples is computed. Then, a (statistics/summary) S-vector representation is derived. The S-vector contains various statistical parameters for each attribute in the results set, such as the minimum, maximum, and average for a numerical attribute or the number of distinct values of a symbolic attribute. The proposed method was evaluated on a real dataset taken from a Web-based application using three different classification algorithms (naïve Bayes, decision tree, and support vector machine). The proposed data-centric approach is here compared to the [Kamra, 2008] syntax-centric approach, with reported accuracy levels ranging from 93% to 96%.

The drawback of the data-centric approach is that the query must be executed before the decision can be made. In addition, the data are assumed to be static and unchanging. If the data do change, retraining is required.

Fonseca et al. (2008) proposed the Malicious Data Access Detector (MDAD), a mechanism for detecting malicious data access through online analysis of the database management systems (DBMS) audit trail. The proposed mechanism aims to protect database applications from data attacks and Web-based applications from SQL-injection types of attacks. This is done by representing the profile of valid transactions by a directed graph which describes different sequences of SQL queries (SELECTs, INSERTs, UPDATEs, and DELETEs) from the beginning of the transaction to the commit or rollback command. The nodes in the graph represent commands, while the arcs represent valid execution sequences. In the detection phase, the mechanism detects transactions that fall outside the learned profile, the DBA is warned, and the malicious session is terminated. It is assumed that the application used to submit queries does not change. The proposed mechanism was implemented and evaluated using an Oracle database. The standard benchmark TPC-C database and a production database were used to assess the detection mechanism and learning algorithm, yielding an accuracy greater than 99%.

Yaseen and Panda (2009) also used a data-centric approach and proposed a method for modeling the knowledge that an insider can infer from a given set of data records.

Given that the insider has legitimate access to tables, attributes and records, she can apply her knowledge to derive new knowledge. The method uses dependency graphs based on domain-expert knowledge. The domain expert defines (1) knowledge of the organization's data-object dependencies (i.e., what additional data can be inferred or calculated from the data presented to the user); (2) the data that are restricted or highly sensitive; and (3) the people within the organization who are permitted to access these data. These graphs are used to predict the ability of a user to infer sensitive information that might harm the organization using information that she has already obtained. The derived knowledge is categorized into three types: inferred, computed, and aggregated. The database object (to which the insider may or may not have access), the basic knowledge, and the derived knowledge are modeled as a neural dependency and inference graph (NDIG) which was inspired by the concept of an artificial neural network. The NDIG presents the data objects, the dependencies between data objects, and the amount of knowledge that the insider can infer given knowledge about prior data objects. The NDIG model may assist in understanding the potential damage that an insider can cause by using her legitimate access rights and applying her knowledge of the system and domain in an unauthorized manner. Using the NDIG model, the system can prevent unauthorized users from gaining information which enables them to infer or to calculate restricted data which they are not eligible to access.

Other studies have dealt with intrusion detection in databases rather than focusing on data leakage. This research usually takes the syntax-based approach and targets the maintenance of data integrity by detecting anomalous transactions including INSERTs and UPDATEs. These systems are less relevant for detecting data misuse or leakage than those discussed previously, but the concepts applied in these systems might be useful for implementing an innovative leakage prevention solution [Chung, 1999], [Valeur, 2005], [Hu, 2004], [Hu, 2003], [Spalka, 2005], [Srivastava, 2006], [Wenhui, 2001], [Lee, 2000], and [Lee, 2002].

4.2.3 Email leakage protection

Research in this field can be divided into two main categories: content-based approaches and behavior-based approaches.

The content-based approach for detecting and preventing data leakage can be further divided into:

- **keywords-based rules**. In this approach, various rules are retrieved from keywords that appear in the body and the header of an email. These rules determine the "confidentiality level" of the scanned email based on the number of appearances of certain keywords [Cohen, 1996], [Helfman, 1995] and [Rennie, 2000].
- **machine learning techniques**. The basic idea of this approach is to use machine learning techniques such as SVM ([Cohen, 1999], [Drucker, 1999]) and naïve Bayes ([Androutsopoulos, 2000], [Hovold, 2005], and [Sahami, 1998]) to determine the "confidentiality level" of the scanned email message.

Two methods are used to represent textual data in emails. The first method is the *vector space model*. Vectors represent documents, and vector features represent terms and their frequency of appearance [Salton, 1986]. The vectors are used as learning sets to build a probabilistic model, on the basis of which decisions are made whether or not documents are confidential.

The second method for the representation of textual data is *graphs*. In general, words are represented as nodes in the graph and are connected by edges to words that appear in their vicinity. Schenker (2003) presented six major groups of algorithms for creating graphs from document text: simple, *n*-simple distance, standard, *n*-distance, relative frequency, and absolute frequency. The algorithms differ in their use of term-based techniques, for example the representation of the order of words appearing in the document, the representation of the distance between words (up to a certain predefined distance), and whether the frequencies of appearance of two or more terms together should be calculated. Graph-based document representation methods can capture the structure of the document as well as its content, which vector-based representation methods do not.

The behavior-based approach focuses on environment-related features such as organizational structure and which users send and receive email. For example, in [Kalyan, 2007], the likelihood that an email has been sent by mistake is determined based on an analysis of past communications between email senders and recipients.

In [Carvalho, 2007], a sent email is identified as a leak based on the textual content of the email and the likelihood that the recipient of the email should be receiving it. Messages sent to past recipients are modeled as (message, recipient) pairs, and a (message, recipient) pair is considered to be a potential leak if the message is sufficiently different from past messages sent to that recipient. To improve performance, Carvalho and Cohen (2007) used various social network features.

Their proposed solution used two different techniques for detection. The first technique relies strictly on the message's textual content. It measures the similarity between two vector-based representations of email messages. The first vector is a TF-IDF representation of all previous messages from the current user u to recipient r (a different vector is created for each recipient). The second vector is a TF-IDF representation of the current message which is about to be sent. The distance between the two vectors is measured using one of two suggested algorithms: cosine-similarity or k-nearest neighbors (KNN). If the computed similarity is less than a predefined threshold, a warning message is issued to the user who is about to send the message. This comparison is done separately for each recipient of the message which is about to be sent.

The second technique proposed was a classification-based method and was implemented using social network information (such as the number of received messages, the number of sent messages, and the number of times that a particular pair of recipients were copied in the same message). The idea was to perform leak prediction in two steps. In the first step, textual similarity scores were calculated using a cross-validation procedure on the training set. In the second step, network features were extracted, and then a function which combined these features with textual scores was calculated.

To test the proposed method, email leaks were simulated on the basis of the Enron email corpus[1] using different possible criteria. These criteria imitate realistic types of leaks, such as misspellings of email addresses, typos, similar first/last names, etc. This method was able to detect almost 82% of the test cases as email leaks. The advantage of this approach is that it can be easily implemented in an email client and does not use any information which is available to the server only.

In a later study, Carvalho et al. (2009) presented an implementation of their solution on Mozilla Thunderbird. They also expanded their system not only to detect undesired recipients, but also to suggest recipients that the user might have failed to include. This solution suggested installing a plug-in into the existing Mozilla Thunderbird engine. The evaluation of this study showed unpromising results. Only 15% of the users reported that the client prevented real occurrences of email leaks, and more than 47% of them accepted the recommendations provided by the data mining techniques. On the other hand, more than 80% of the subjects participating in the test case reported they would use this solution in their email clients on an ongoing basis if a few interface and optimization improvements were implemented.

4.2.4 Network/web-based protection

Borders and Prakash (2008) described a method for quantifying potential network-based information leaks. This approach uses the fact that a large portion of network traffic is repeated or constrained by protocol specifications. By ignoring these fixed data, the true information that flows from a client to the Internet can be isolated. The authors focused on the Hypertext Transfer Protocol (HTTP) and computed the content of expected HTTP requests using only externally available information, including previous network requests, previous server responses, and protocol specifications. This resulted in a measurement of the amount of unrepeated and unconstrained outbound bandwidth that represents the maximum amount of information that could have been leaked by the client. These leak quantification techniques were evaluated on Web traffic from several legitimate Web-browsing scenarios. The evaluation results showed that the new algorithm produced request size measurements that were 94% to 99.7% smaller than the raw bandwidth values, which demonstrated the ability of this approach to filter out constrained information and to isolate true information flows that should be inspected, thus reducing the network traffic inspection time required. The authors stated that this approach cannot handle malicious Web requests from pages with active Javascript code or Flash objects.

Caputo et al. (2009) presented the Elicit system that monitors users' access to information on an intranet. The system uses network-based sensors that process network traffic to produce information-use events such as searching, browsing,

---

[1] http://www.cs.cmu.edu/enron

reading, deleting, and printing. The collected events are combined with contextual information and processed by various rule-based and statistical detectors that may issue alerts. Finally, alerts from detectors are fed into a Bayesian network which produces a probability that a user's activity is malicious.

4.2.5   Encryption and access control

Encryption and access control are two of the most common means for preventing leakage of confidential data through access restriction. Such frameworks use access control and encryption to secure sensitive data at-rest (e.g., stored on laptops, servers, PCs, etc.), in-motion (e.g. transferred through the local network or on the Web), and in-use (being accessed or modified).

Access control mechanisms in place can reduce the risk of data leakage; however, the amount of reduction is still limited because legitimate users such as employees and partners continue to have access to sensitive data. Several related studies have addressed this issue.

One of the key questions in solutions that provide encryption of data or even of the whole disk (for example TrueCrypt) is how encryption will affect data recovery in cases where the password has been forgotten or in the context of incident investigation and forensics [Forte, 2009].

Abbadi and Alawneh (2008) presented a solution for preventing information leakage when the adversary is someone who is authorized to view the data. Generally, the proposed framework allows authorized users access to sensitive information from inside or outside an organization's premises (access from outside the organization is over VPN). The key concept is allowing access to sensitive data on authorized devices only and protecting sensitive data from unauthorized disclosure. This is achieved by creating a domain of devices which are authorized to access the data. Each domain has its own specific master controller that manages security administrator authentication, secure addition and removal of devices to and from the domain, and domain-specific key distribution (denoted as KD). Only devices inside the organization's premises are authorized to join the domain: otherwise, they cannot own a KD. The joining device has to be trusted, i.e., to correspond to the expected state of the device, and must be physically added by an authenticated security administrator. The only entity on a device that is authorized to manage encryption keys is a trusted software agent, who is assumed to use hardware that provides cryptographic functions.

While being transferred between domain devices, sensitive data are encrypted using the domain key KD. Because the KD key can be transferred only from the trusted master controller to an authorized device, it is stored in a protected storage area and cannot be copied between devices. This guarantees that if sensitive data reaches an unauthorized device, they cannot be disclosed.

While being stored in a device, the sensitive data are encrypted using a device-specific key, denoted as KC. KC is stored in a protected storage area. Before data are transferred, they are decrypted using KC and re-encrypted using KD.

This framework prevents unprotected data from being transferred using the Web or mass data storage (assumed to be prevented by the trusted software agent). It also prevents access to sensitive data on unauthorized devices. However, the proposed framework does not prevent an authorized user from rendering content on an authorized device with the physical presence of another unauthorized user (assuming that physical controls are not in place). It also does not prevent an authorized user from memorizing, writing, or recording content and then transferring it to others.

Alawneh and Abbadi (2008) further described a framework for protecting sensitive data shared between collaborating organizations. In such cases, one organization required sensitive data from another organization, but the data still needed to be protected from leakage to unauthorized users inside or outside the destination organization. The proposed solution is based on *trusted computing*, which provides a hardware-based root of trust. The shared data are protected while being sent to the collaborating organization by establishing VPN connections. Definitions of global domains in the destination organization ensure that the data can be shared between devices in the domain while still remaining protected from leakage outside the organization. The trusted computing platform ensures that the data are kept encrypted and that the encryption key is accessible only to devices in the domain and cannot be transferred to devices outside the organization. A software agent installed on the device will refuse to release sensitive content to other devices unprotected (even if they are a member of the global domain). Dynamic domains are used to specify subgroups of devices, which should be the only ones to share content using the domain-specific key.

Parno et al. (2009) presented CLAMP (Confidential Linux Apache MySQL PHP applications), which is a transformation performed on top of an existing LAMP-based Web application and which results in a more data-leak-proof application. The transformation is based on taking the authentication process out of the application boundaries into a separate user authenticator (UA) module. In addition, each user who connects to the server will get a fresh and clean duplication of the server (called WebStack) forked from a protected unchangeable copy. The new WebStack runs in a separate virtual memory area, which provides total isolation between the servers serving each user, and which in turn means that damage to one server instance will not affect the rest of the servers. The WebStack ID and the single unique UA which is attached to it are used by the *query restrictor* (QR). The QR is a database proxy that creates a "virtual" database (using the database's "view" capability) which contains only the data that the user is allowed to see and which restricts SELECT, INSERT, and UPDATE operations according to a predefined policy. The authors claimed that it is relatively easy to modify an existing Web application to work with CLAMP. On the other hand, the method consumes large amounts of memory and CPU resources on the server and cannot protect against insider attack.

Yasuhiro and Yoshik (2002) presented a Web-based framework aimed at preventing leakage of confidential information. This is done by encrypting confidential data and granting access only to authorized users, as well as by using a specialized viewer embedded in the Internet browser for decrypting and viewing content. The system operates in two phases: the download phase and the viewing phase. The download phase is based on a smart proxy that uses an authorization database to determine whether the current user can download the requested content and whether the content needs to be encrypted before sending it through. In the viewing phase, a smart viewer on the user's computer handles the request for the decryption key and decrypts the content. Following decryption, the smart viewer presents the content to the user (allowing the user to view the content once per key download), and the viewer is able to disable the save, print, and print-screen operations. The proposed framework is transparent to the user and protects confidential data while they are at-rest (encrypted in the database), in-motion (being sent encrypted over the network), and in-use (the user can watch the content in a specialized viewer that prohibits printing or saving). However, the print-screen option is not completely blocked and can be bypassed.

The concept of fine-grained access control for database systems was initially proposed to provide better data protection by controlling access at the granularity level of individual rows and columns [Kabra, 2006]. Fine-grained access control at the database level (as opposed to the application program level) can be provided by modifying the query by appending predicates to the WHERE clause of the query or by modifying the original table being accessed by injecting a dynamically created temporary view between the query and the target table [Zhu, 2008].

De Capitani Di Vimercati et al. (2010) proposed the concept of selective encryption to provide selective access control to outsourced sensitive data by third-party partners. According to the proposed approach the data access authorization policy is processed to compute a hierarchical structure of tokens which are used to derive a set of cryptographic keys. This set of cryptographic keys, referred to as an encryption policy, enables selective encryption of and access to the data. The authors proved that the problem of computing a minimum encryption policy is NP-hard and presented a heuristic algorithm to solve the problem.

4.2.6   Hidden data in files

Documents written and stored in the Microsoft Word document format might contain hidden data. However, awareness of this problem is not sufficiently widespread, especially among non-technical computer users [Byers, 2004]. Examples of hidden data in Word documents include the names and usernames of the document's creators and their collaborators and organizational information on the users involved.

Yixiang et al. (2007) claimed that publishing an XML document data with security requirements poses a multitude of challenges when users can infer data using common knowledge. Moreover, when two or more documents are involved, users can infer the sensitive data by combining the documents. The core of the Eliminate Inner Nodes algorithm, for use when publishing several related XML documents, is to find a maximal partial document which avoids information leakage while at the same time allows for publishing as much data as possible.

4.2.7 Honeypots for detecting malicious insiders

A honeypot is a mechanism which is commonly used for detecting attacks from an outside source. It is an artificial resource set up as a trap which is aimed at detecting, deflecting, or in some sense counteracting attempts at unauthorized use of information systems. Generally, the trap consists of a computer, database, Web site, or application server that appears to be part of a real production network, but is actually isolated, intentionally unprotected, and unobtrusively monitored. The honeypot should look genuine, be available, and be vulnerable to draw the attacker who attempts to exploit it into the trap. Any interaction with the honeypot is by definition an anomalous situation that should be further reported and investigated. Forensic information provided by the honeypot is logged and analyzed to gain insight into various attack patterns (e.g., who the attacker is; where, how, and when was an attack launched; etc.) The collected data enable inspection of attacks at various levels of abstraction, ranging from low-level network interface and routing protocols to higher application-level protocols [Valli, 2005].

Spitzner (2003) noted the following main advantages of honeypots. First, honeypots collect data only when someone or something malicious interacts with them. This makes the data collected by the honeypots highly succinct, accurate, easy to manage, and simple to analyze. Second, honeypots can identify and capture new attacks. Because any activity with the honeypot is anomalous by definition, new or unseen attacks are detectable and result in a low false negative rate.

Honeypots usually focus on intercepting external attacks which attempt to compromise or penetrate a host or network. There are currently only a handful of academic articles on using honeypots to tackle insider threats. These studies discuss two kinds of honeypots: honeytokens and honeyfiles. Honeytokens are fake digital data (e.g., a credit card number, a database entry, or bogus login credentials) planted into a genuine system resource (e.g., a database, a file or an email message). Honeyfiles are files that contain fake information and that are planted in an organization's file system or in a personal folder (e.g., a PowerPoint presentation, an Excel spreadsheet, or an email message).

Internal attackers pose a much greater challenge to organizations because they narrow the detection window available for existing countermeasures such as IDS, firewalls, and IPS. Valli (2005) asserted that more stringent assumptions should be made when using honeypots against insider threats, for example: an insider's legitimate access privileges; existence of high-speed network connections and access to the honeypot; deep acquaintance with the defense configuration and its weaknesses; and knowledge of earlier states of the application architecture, technologies, and functionalities.

The concept of monitoring honeytokens has already been proposed by Storey (2009). According to Storey, the first step is to learn how data items are legitimately used and moved around the organizational network. With this knowledge, honeytokens can be planted into genuine system resources. Using tools such as Snort, these honeytokens can then be monitored.

Spitzner (2003) proposed a two-stage approach for using honeypots. The first stage is planting honeytokens (i.e., user names, passwords) in an organization's applications, files, network traffic, etc. This information can then direct the insider to a more sophisticated honeypot which can be further monitored and can be used to gather information on the perpetrator, to validate whether an insider has malicious or unauthorized intent, and to identify who the insider actually is and perhaps to determine his or her motives. For example, a honeytoken can be inserted into network traffic (e.g., a username and password which will be sent as part of an email text). If a sophisticated insider is passively monitoring network activity, he or she will encounter this honeytoken, which will point to a honeypot application into which the attacker will attempt to login using the honeytoken he or she just obtained.

Following this line of thought, Bowen et al. (2009a) presented the Decoy Document Distributor proof-of-concept system. The Decoy Document Distributor (DDD) system is a Web-based service which first generates and sends decoy documents with embedded honeytokens to registered users and then monitors any activity using the honeytokens. Multiple decoys are sent to increase the detection rate. An example of a honeytoken deployed by D^3 is a fake banking login account specifically created, published, and monitored to attract and trap financially motivated attackers. The detection mechanisms used by the D^3 system can be deployed at the network level, host level, or both to detect the decoy documents. The authors of the decoy documents can be alerted whenever such a document is detected. For example, D^3 will create a MS Word file containing login details for a Gmail bait account. The user downloads this file from the Web server to his laptop. When an attacker notices this file, he will try to login to the bait account. Custom scripts will gather account activity information, and an alert will be triggered. The honeyfiles created by the D^3 system can be monitored by the Decoy Documents Access sensor [Salem, 2011b] for masquerade attack (identity theft) detection. The efficiency of using honeyfiles and the significant effect of the number of honeyfiles and their selected locations were demonstrated in [Salem, 2011b].

In [Čenys, 2005], the authors describe a honeytoken module for an Oracle 9iR2 DBMS which is capable of detecting internal malicious activities. The strategy is to insert a honeytable, namely a table with a "sweet" name such as "CREDIT_CARDS" to attract malicious user.

One of the main challenges in using honeytokens is to create honeytokens that are indistinguishable from real, genuine tokens. A method for creating honeytokens which represent human entities (like employees and customers) is proposed in [White, 2010]. The focus of this method is to create honeytokens which look like realistic records and which contain identifiable attributes such as names, addresses, social security numbers, phone numbers, email addresses, and so on. To generate such tokens, relevant statistics for each attribute were gathered (including a set of potential values and their frequencies), and the dependencies between different fields in the same record were identified. Based on this knowledge, a program was developed to generate honeytokens.

A closely related approach is identifying and monitoring critical (highly sensitive) data items. White and Panda (2009) implemented a statistical data relationship model to locate critical data items. This method attempts to identify data items which have the greatest influence on other data items in the database. The influence of an item is defined by the number of items which are affected by a change in its value. The proposed solution automatically identifies critical data items in a database by scanning database logs and deriving data dependency relationships. These relationships are represented as disjoint directed graphs showing which items influence a larger number of other items and at what frequency this influence occurs. The main purpose of the proposed model is to help database owners focus their security efforts on those critical data items that require extra security measures. Another method of data misuse detection was proposed by White and Panda (2010), in which data items are selected for monitoring according to a criticality score. This score is calculated using explicit rules (provided by experts) and an SVM-based filtering system which is trained on both critical and noncritical data items (i.e., a supervised learner). As a result, the suggested criticality score is based on the sensitivity of the content of the data item.

Papadimitriou and Garcia (2010) presented a method for data leakage detection. In their scenario, a dataset owner distributes *sensitive data objects* to several agents according to specific requests issued by each agent. If the sensitive data are leaked, the data owner would like to be able to identify the source of leakage, or at least to estimate the probability that each agent was involved in the incident. Therefore, a guilt model is proposed for estimating the probability that an agent is involved in a given data leakage incident. The ability to identify the source of the leakage depends on the distribution of data objects among agents. Therefore, a data allocation method, which distributes data records among the agents based on each agent's requests, and an optimization models are presented. The proposed allocation method ensures that sharing of objects among agents is minimal and that therefore, in the case of a leakage incident, the data owner will be able to use the proposed guilt model to identify the source of the leakage with high probability.

Two types of data requests are considered in [Papadimitriou, 2010]: explicit requests and sample requests. An *explicit request* contains specific conditions, and all the objects in the dataset that comply with these conditions must be returned. A *sample request* defines a number of objects to be randomly selected from the entire dataset. Combined requests (i.e., requests for a sample of objects that comply with a specified condition) are not handled by the proposed algorithms; however, the authors explain how they might be handled.

The authors also proposed adding fake data objects to the lists of real data objects when distributing them to the agents. Fake data objects may help to distinguish more effectively between the agents and to increase the accuracy of the guilt model, e.g., when each agent receives a unique fake object.

Four scenarios can be defined by the two request types (sample or explicit) and the two options of planting fake objects in the result sets (using or not using fake objects). It is assumed that in each scenario, all agents issue the same type of requests (i.e., either explicit or sample queries) and that if fake objects are being used, the same number of objects will be planted for all agents. Several allocation algorithms were proposed to deal with each scenario. Empirical evaluation showed that the proposed algorithms had a significantly greater ability to identify the source of leakage than simple allocation algorithms, even in cases with a large overlap between the sets of objects that the agents received.

Chapter 5
Data Leakage/Misuse Scenarios

5.1 Classification of data leakage/misuse scenarios

Data leakage incidents can be characterized based on the following attributes: where the leakage occurred, who caused the leakage, what was leaked (data state), how was access to the data gained, and how did the data leak. These parameters affect decision making for data-leakage defense measures.

5.1.1 Where did the leakage occur?

Three possible leakage locations are distinguished here: *inside the organization* – data were leaked from a source residing within the organization's physical perimeter; *outside the organization* – data were leaked from an external source residing outside the organization's perimeter (e.g., a laptop was stolen from an employee's car); and *third-party location* – data were leaked from a trusted third-party location (e.g., a partner's network was hacked and its credentials were used to access the data).

5.1.2 Who caused the leakage?

Security incidents may originate from one or more of the following sources: an insider, an outsider, a contractor/vendor, or a consumer/customer. Franqueira et al. (2010) categorized leakage sources as outsiders, insiders, and external insiders (third partners, contractors, vendors, customers, etc.) and discussed the challenges in detecting insiders and external insiders.

Most *insiders* are trusted to a certain degree, and some possess high levels of access privileges (IT administrators and DBAs in particular). Insiders can be further distinguished based on the nature of the action that led to the data leakage,

A. Shabtai et al., *A Survey of Data Leakage Detection and Prevention Solutions*,
SpringerBriefs in Computer Science, DOI 10.1007/978-1-4614-2053-8_5,
© The Author(s) 2012

i.e., whether it was accidental or intentional. *Outsiders* (e.g., hackers, organized crime groups, and government entities) are typically not trusted individuals, and no privileges are provided or delegated to them. *Third-party partners* such as contractors, vendors, and suppliers usually share a business relationship with the organization and are known as the extended enterprise. Information exchange is the lifeblood of the extended enterprise, and therefore some level of trust and privilege is usually implied between business partners. These relationships are facilitated using technologies such as extranets, VPNs, and encryption. *Consumers and customers* are often granted privileges to use specific applications or services.

5.1.3 What was leaked?

Both DLP solution providers and academic researchers distinguish between three phases of data throughout their lifecycle: data-at-rest (DAR), data-in-motion (DIM), and data-in-use (DIU). Different approaches are used to protect data in different phases of their lifecycle. Incidents should be classified according to the data state that existed when control over the data was lost. Note that each incident may be classified into more than one data state.

5.1.4 How was access to the data gained?

The "How was access to the data gained?" attribute extends the "Who caused the leak?" attribute. These attributes are not interchangeable, but rather complementary, and the various ways to gain access to sensitive data can be clustered into the following groups.

- *Hacking*: this term includes exploiting shared or default credentials (e.g., the administrator user of the database which was created by default upon installation and was never changed), exploiting misconfigured access control mechanisms or a system backdoor to bypass authentication and to gain direct access to sensitive data, using stolen legitimate credentials, gaining access to sensitive data or credentials using SQL injection, cross-site scripting (XSS), stolen session variables, and buffer overflow attacks.
- *Malware*: may potentially lead to intentional or ingenuous data leakage, for example by recording keystrokes which include usernames and passwords, opening a backdoor to an attacker, or simply sending accessible data over the network. A malware can be installed inside the organization by an attacker, by an employee browsing on unsafe sites across the Internet, or by executing a malware file received as an email attachment, releasing a worm which propagates by exploiting system vulnerabilities or by physical propagation using removable media [Menahem, 2009].

- *Social attacks*: come in the form of observation or shoulder surfing, assault or threat of harm, dumpster diving, and social engineering.
- *Physically accessing* the machine (or media) where the sensitive data reside, bypassing any network protection mechanisms. This includes theft or loss of the asset (e.g., a laptop), interacting with the system through a keyboard, and wiretapping (i.e., monitoring a network cable, Wi-Fi transmission, phone line or any other transport protocol over which sensitive may pass).
- *Human errors*: includes errors by developers, IT professionals, or data owners, including misconfiguration, programming errors, saving sensitive information on a server that is exposed to the Web, and improper disposal of sensitive documents or electronic media such as CD/DVDs.

5.1.5 How did the data leak?

The classification by leakage channel is important to determine how incidents may be prevented in the future.

Physical leakage channel: physical media (e.g., HDDs, laptops, workstations, CD/DVDs, USB devices) which contain sensitive information or the document itself were moved outside the organization. This more than often means that control over the data was lost even before they left the organization.

Logical leakage channel: refers to scenarios in which data are leaked in the form of digital information, or in other words broadcast, uploaded, or sent outside the organization using the capabilities of its applications and computer networks. This includes Web uploads (i.e., information was uploaded to a remote destination such as a file server, a Web site, a mail server using Web-mail, etc.), Web application abuse, storage on exposed locations on the Web, instant messaging (Skype, ICQ, MS Messenger, etc.), third-party applications (P2P), and malware (i.e., unknown protocol).

5.2 Description of main data leakage/misuse scenarios

A list of the main data-leakage scenario groups is presented in Table 5.1. Each scenario may include both intentional and unintentional incidents. For example, an unintentional situation might involve the theft or loss of a physical device and its improper disposal (throwing a hard drive with sensitive data into the garbage), while an intentional case might involve an employee stealing a company hard drive full of sensitive data. The end result for both cases is similar; the hard drive's data become compromised.

However, when evaluating solutions to these scenarios, it has been found that solutions often differ greatly between the two cases and that often the intentional case is harder to mitigate. Figure 5.1 provides a summary review of various leakage

Table 5.1 Main groups of data leakage scenarios

	Scenario	Description
1	Mass storage device is physically lost or stolen	Company's sensitive information is stored on a mass storage device which is lost, stolen, or improperly disposed of, resulting in the information being exposed to unauthorized entities. Examples of such media include: desktops, laptops, HDDs, CDs/DVDs, backup tapes and other electronic media. This scenario can be caused by an insider with legitimate physical access to these media and who may steal or duplicate the sensitive data stored on them, or by an outside attacker stealing the device while it is temporarily not on the organization's premises.
2	Third-party company leaks sensitive data	A partner sells sensitive data (e.g., customers' phone numbers, names, and contract details), potentially to competitor companies. Alternatively, a third-party vendor (i.e., an outsourcing subcontractor) may accidentally expose sensitive data.
3	Illegal storage of data on other systems/ devices/media	An employee stores sensitive data on other devices, e.g., his or her personal home desktop, laptop, USB device, CD/DVD, or a network storage that does not belong to the company (e.g., Gmail).
4	Stolen identity/shared credentials	The identity of an employee is stolen or passed on to another unauthorized person and is later used to access sensitive information. Includes passing smartcards, sharing passwords, and leaving a computer unlocked while unattended.
5	Misuse of privileges	An employee (DBA, Admin) misuses legitimate privileges and ability to access sensitive data beyond the scope of his or her work assignments.
6	Public sharing of data	An employee accidentally grants access to sensitive data stored on his or her machine through file sharing and communication applications (P2P, IM, etc.), or accidently places sensitive data in a publicly accessed location (e.g. a Web server).
7	Email leakage	An employee sends an email message with the wrong attachment or to the wrong recipient, leaking sensitive information.
8	Hacker gains access to sensitive data	A hacker gains access to workstations or servers and steals sensitive data. Alternatively, the hacker gains access to an internal database by hacking a Web application or by injecting scripts or SQL statements (i.e., SQL injection).
9	Virus/malware steals data	A computer virus or malware is used to steal sensitive data which are then transmitted over the Web. Generally, an updated antivirus utility will detect instances of known malware and remove them. This is not the case with zero-day malware or target-specific, isolated Trojan-horse malware, which might evade detection.
10	Hidden sensitive data inside files	An employee uses a sensitive file as a template (e.g., an Excel sheet containing customers' private information) and deletes the sensitive data part; however, use of the "track changes" feature means that the sensitive data were not really deleted.

(continued)

Table 5.1 (continued)

	Scenario	Description
11	Illegal export of sensitive data from a controlled system	Sensitive data (e.g., customer data) can be exported or copied to a file from a control system (e.g., a CRM). It is assumed that once such data leave the controlled system, protecting them from leaking out becomes a much harder task. Therefore, solutions which prevent the data from illegally leaving the controlled systems should be in place. In some cases, the data are legally exported (for example, to generate a report containing statistical information). If exporting the data is legal and should not be prevented, the data might still leak out, for example, if the report were sent to a wrong recipient with an email message or stored on a USB stick which is lost. However, such cases are beyond the scope of this scenario and have been addressed by scenarios mentioned earlier.

	Device control	Encryption	Monitor DIM	Monitor DIU	Scan DAR	RMS-based access control	Activity-based auth. and verification	Two-factor auth.	Anomaly detection	Detect email leaks using ML	Honeypots
11. Exported data from controlled systems				●●	●●						
10. Hidden data in files			●●	●●	●●						
9. Malware			●	●							
8. Hacking			●	●							●
7. Email leak			●●	●●		●●				●●	
6. Public sharing of data	●●		●●	●●	●●	●●					
5. Misuse of privileges	●			●	●				●		●
4. Stolen/Shared identity	●●		●●	●●				●●	●●	●●	
3. Illegal storage in other systems	●●		●●	●●		●●					
2. Partner leaks data						●●					●●
1. Device physically stolen/lost	●●	●●		●●	●●						
	Device control	Encryption	Monitor DIM	Monitor DIU	Scan DAR	RMS-based access control	Activity-based auth. and verification	Two-factor auth.	Anomaly detection	Detect email leaks using ML	Honeypots

Fig. 5.1 Mapping of applicable data leakage/misuse prevention solutions for various leakage/misuse scenarios

solutions with regard to the scenarios presented in Table 5.1. For each scenario (listed on the Y-axis), the effectiveness of the various solutions was qualitatively estimated (as shown on the X-axis) for the intentional (black icons) and unintentional cases (gray icons). For example, the ● symbol indicates a highly effective solution, while the ◔ symbol indicates an ineffective solution.

The following paragraphs present a discussion of the various means for tackling each of the scenarios listed.

For scenario 1 (*device physically stolen/lost*), it is harder to prevent sensitive data from residing on the device than simply to encrypt the entire disk, and therefore encryption provides near-total protection. However, encryption alone is not sufficient and should be used in combination with device control (to ensure that data are transferred only to encrypted devices) and with other designated DLP products which monitor DIU and DAR. In addition, the ability to prove that sensitive data were encrypted and thereby protected on a lost or stolen device is important to the organization from a regulatory compliance perspective.

Scenario 2 (*partner leaks data*) is hard to detect or prevent because it involves a third party that cannot be easily monitored. RMS-based access control offers some degree of control over data security and is generally effective against unintentional leaks by third parties because an RMS tool prevents data from being copied beyond the perimeter of the RMS framework and limits access to authorized parties only. A malicious user may use the print-screen function or a hard copy of the data to bypass the RMS protection framework. Honeypots can also be an effective mechanism for detecting leaks by third-party companies because the leak is exposed the moment that the fake data are acted upon (e.g., calling up a fake customer). In any case, honeypots used to detect insiders must be constructed and used wisely.

Scenario 3 (*illegal storage on other systems*) deals with storage of sensitive data on unauthorized devices like home laptops and USB sticks or in unauthorized locations like personal blogs, Wikis, forums, Gmail, etc. Standard DLP solutions that monitor DIM and DIU offer solid protection (within the envelope of their detection abilities) because they can monitor sensitive data and prevent them from being posted on the Web or transferred to external devices. Standard DLP solutions are, however, ineffective against a malicious user who intentionally attempts to take data outside the organization using the Web or a portable device (e.g., a USB stick) because such a user will eventually find a way to bypass the detection system (for example, by encrypting the file). Device control can be used to limit the user's ability to transfer data to unapproved devices, and furthermore, applying RMS encryption to the sensitive data can help maintain protection even if data are leaked and stored in other systems.

For scenario 4 (*stolen/shared identity*), standard DLP solutions for monitoring DIM and DIU offer a certain amount of protection in that, they will act to prevent any detected leaks regardless of the person(s) involved. However, they do not prevent access to data by a malicious impersonator who can easily bypass the detection mechanisms provided by these solutions. Solutions such as activity-based authentication, which can detect whenever a user behaves abnormally (e.g., by different keystroke patterns), or other anomaly-detection mechanisms (i.e., based on database query/document access patterns) offer potential for protection in both intentional and unintentional cases. Unfortunately, these solutions are not always applicable and may cause a large number of false alarms. Use of two factor authentication process has been found to be effective for both intentional and unintentional scenarios and will in addition act as a significant barrier which an impersonator must bypass.

Scenario 5 (*misuse of privileges*) involves a legitimate user who uses access to sensitive data in an inappropriate manner. This is a difficult scenario to detect and to protect against. Anomaly detection may provide some protection under this scenario because it can detect abnormal access to data by a privileged user (for example, by detecting abnormal database queries). However, if the user is aware of this mechanism, he or she can possibly bypass it by issuing smart and "stealthy" queries. Honeypots can assist in detecting some of these incidents as they occur, but offer little in terms of prevention. Device control and monitoring DIU and DIM may restrict the user's ability to transport data outside the organization, but the privileged user may find ways to circumvent these restrictions.

Scenario 6 (*public sharing of data*) refers mostly to detection of unintentional leaks by means of intentional leaks by users, who often take advantage of these functions as a means to export sensitive data. Standard DLP solutions and monitoring DAR, DIU, and DIM offer effective protection under this scenario. These solutions will detect and block transmission of sensitive data stored in public locations. Encryption and RMS techniques increase security because sensitive data remain protected (encrypted) even after being shared.

Scenario 7 (*email leak*) is a scenario of highly critical importance because information is unintentionally exposed by insecure email communication (i.e., wrong attachments, wrong addressees, CC instead of BCC, etc.) Existing DLP solutions can scan emails for sensitive data in text or attachments (within the current boundaries of their detection abilities) and then block or redirect the sensitive data to special handling by encryption add-ons. RMS encryption can be applied to sensitive data before they are attached to an email to maintain control of these data even outside organization boundaries. Leakage incidents can also be prevented by learning a user's email-exchange patterns using machine learning (ML) techniques, such as identifying an email which is about to be sent to a wrong recipient.

Scenarios 8 and 9 (*hacking and malware*) are both malicious and intentional attacks, and current solutions offer little protection against such scenarios. DIM monitoring can scan outbound communications and block sensitive data from leaving a company's edge gateway. However, a skilled hacker might craft a special malware instance capable of evading such detection (for example, by altering the data to make them appear not to be sensitive). Encryption of data offers reasonable protection because even if an attacker has gained access to the data, they are still protected. Hacking can be detected by deploying honeypots in addition to other general security solutions such as antivirus and firewalls.

For scenario 10 (*hidden data in files*), existing DLP solutions use content extraction engines that extract all the contents of a file, including hidden data, for deep inspection (i.e., checking a Word document's metadata which are managed by MS Office). Within the boundaries of the detection ability available in these solutions, a leak will be prevented.

Scenario 11 (*exported data from controlled systems*) is viewed as a security breach because it overrides and bypasses the authority in charge of the data, and the data in turn become more prone to leakage. It is possible to prevent a leak once the data are at large using the various solutions mentioned in this report; however, this is much harder compared to a situation where the data reside inside the owner's organization. Existing DLP products that monitor DIU can interact with sensitive applications and monitor specific components and windows of these applications to prevent specified dangerous actions such as copying and pasting sensitive data. DAR scanning can detect data that have "escaped" the control system, but should still be protected.

5.3   Discussion

Figure 5.1 indicates that a combination of the main functionalities provided by commercial DLP products, monitoring data-in-motion, monitoring data-in-use, and scanning data-at-rest, can reduce the risk of most accidental leakage scenarios. Current solutions, however, do not provide sufficient protection against intentional attacks. Protection from intentional attacks can be partially achieved using a standard RMS access control framework and other innovative solutions such as activity-based verification and authentication, anomaly detection (aimed at detecting data misuse), and honeypots. Moreover, improving the methods for detecting sensitive data can increase the effectiveness of existing commercial DLP products.

Additional "non-designated" DLP solutions currently available on the market are also relevant and can be useful for detecting or preventing leakages as one of their auxiliary functions. Thin clients can be used to control sensitive information and to ensure that it remains stored in a central location and not on local unregulated hosts. Workstation management techniques can be used to apply data-handling policies accompanied by technological measures which prevent the installation of third-party or unapproved applications (e.g., file sharing) on company computers. Common security tools such as anti-malware software, intrusion detection systems, and firewalls also provide assistance in detecting malicious software or intrusion attempts.

Another approach to minimizing unintentional leakage risks is by defining and enforcing policies, standards, regulations, and guidelines. Defining a blueprint for data protection, along with raising employee awareness (by means of security lectures, signing of nondisclosure agreements, etc.) can be very effective in reducing the number of unintentional leakage incidents. Some DLP vendors (e.g., McAfee) issue an informative user alert (in a pop-up window) when a leakage incident is detected (e.g., an attempt to copy sensitive data to a USB device) in an effort to train the user. Such policies usually define both technical and administrative measures. Some examples of technical measures are: all laptops must be equipped with smart-card and encryption capabilities; two-factor authentication must be used on systems holding sensitive data; updated anti-malware utility software must be installed on every PC; installation of unapproved applications must be prevented. Some examples of administrative measures are: laptops should not be left unattended in cars; unused media should be properly destroyed; customer data should not be uploaded to an unprotected or public storage location; strong passwords must be enforced; passwords should never be stored near the computer and should never be passed to others.

Chapter 6
Privacy, Data Anonymization, and Secure Data Publishing

6.1 Introduction to data anonymization

Data anonymization aims to mitigate privacy and security concerns and to comply with legal requirements by obfuscating personal details [Fung, 2010]. In this way, data anonymization prevents an adversary from mapping sensitive information to an individual. There are three primary circumstances in which data anonymization is required:

Data Sharing: Anonymization is required before sensitive data (e.g., customers' private data) are exposed, so that the data can be analyzed without revealing or exposing private information. A data owner may wish to allow third parties to perform analysis and mining on the data she owns. For example, a pharmaceutical company may wish to identify consumption patterns of their products for research purposes. This analysis can be carried out with raw data, but might violate customer privacy. It is therefore necessary to expose only an anonymized version of the data.

Data Usage: Anonymization is on the one hand required to use certain data, but also on the other hand to comply with worldwide data-protection legislation restricting the use of sensitive data. Restrictions refer to the way in which organizations can legally use sensitive data within the organization (for example, testing data in QA environments where new programs are tested). For example, the U.K. Data Protection Act (DPA) essentially prohibits the use of data if an original customer, account, secure entity, or overall data trend can be identified from them. The DPA also requires that companies not use more than the minimum amount of data needed to meet their needs and to make "best efforts" to ensure the accuracy and security of the sensitive data that they do use. There are also industry-specific acts such as the Health Insurance Portability and Accountability Act (HIPAA), the Payment Card Industry Data Security Standard (PCI-DSS), the Markets in Financial Instruments Directive (MIFID), the Gramm-Leach-Bliley Act (GLBA), and the Sarbanes-Oxley Act of 2002 (SOX).

A. Shabtai et al., *A Survey of Data Leakage Detection and Prevention Solutions*, SpringerBriefs in Computer Science, DOI 10.1007/978-1-4614-2053-8_6,

A common example of data usage is extracting production data that include sensitive and private data for testing and QA. The alternatively of using simulated data for testing is usually not a realistic option because the process is time-consuming and expensive. More important, a live database environment must be replicated exactly for accurate testing and development, and using artificial data may limit the effectiveness and validity of the testing. Consequently, the only way to preserve privacy and protect sensitive information at the same time is by masking production data while still maintaining its utility.

Data Retention: Anonymization is required of a company that wishes to retain its data. Retention of private data without data anonymity is restricted by law. For example, Google progressively anonymizes IP addresses in search logs to comply with this requirement.

How can companies protect their private data while still enabling these critical processes? One approach is to require everyone handling the actual production data to sign a confidentiality agreement prohibiting disclosure of sensitive information. However, even with confidentiality agreements, there is no guarantee that the actual production data will remain confidential. One feasible solution might be to anonymize the data before they are exposed.

6.2   Elementary anonymization operations

This section describes elementary operations that can be performed on data to anonymize them. Different models and algorithms use many variations of these operations. Different classes of anonymization operations have different implications for privacy protection, data utility, and search space; however, they all result in a less precise representation of the original data.

6.2.1   Generalization

Generalization of an attribute refers to the replacement of values by more general (less accurate), but still correct values. This, of course, affects the ability to identify unique tuples with specific values. Suppose that the data domain has a natural hierarchical structure. For example, zip codes can be thought of as the leaves of a hierarchy, where 7522* is the parent of 75221 and 752* is the ancestor of 7522*. Using this hierarchy, attributes can be generalized by replacing each original value with that of an ancestor. For example, the values of the attribute "race," which originally come from the set {*Black, White, Asian*}, can be replaced by the generic value {person}. The degree of specification (or generalization) can be measured by the height in the hierarchy of the replacment value. In other words, the higher the place on the hierarchy, the more general is the value. Such a hierarchy is usually referred to as a *taxonomy tree*. Figure 6.1 shows a taxonomy tree of professional

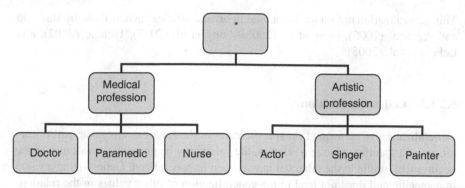

Fig. 6.1 Taxonomy tree

affiliation values. The *Doctor* value is a leaf node; its parent node is *Medical Profession* and *, which means any profession, is the parent node of the medical profession.

Below are several options or schemes for generalization:

6.2.1.1   Full-domain generalization

A taxonomy tree, which is related to the full-domain generalization scheme applied to a table, is a tree in which all the values which appear in the table are taken from the same level or height in the tree. Thus, when generalizing a table according to the full-domain generalization, the generalization is performed in a manner in which all values are generalized to the same level in a taxonomy tree. Consequently, when generalizing, for instance, the leaf value *Doctor* to *Medical Profession* in Figure 6.1, all other leaf values will also be generalized to their corresponding ancestor in that level of the taxonomy tree (*Nurse*, *Paramedic* will be generalized to *Medical Profession* and, *Actor*, *Painter*, and *Singer* will be generalized to *Artistic Profession*). This generalization option has been used by several authors such as LeFevre et al. (2005), Samarati (2001), and Sweeney (2002b).

6.2.1.2   Cut/subtree generalization

A *cut* in a taxonomy tree is characterized by having exactly one value on every root-to-leaf path. Another phrasing for a cut in a taxonomy tree is any selection of disjoint subsets (nodes) from the tree whose union equals the domain of the attribute. When performing generalizations, the cut structure of the tree must remain intact. Thus, for example, when generalizing a value to its parent value, all its sibling values must be generalized to their mutual parent value as well.

Generalizing *Doctor* to *Medical Profession* in Figure 6.1 also requires generalizing any instances of *Nurse* and *Paramedic* to *Medical Profession*. However, other leaf values which are not descendants of *Medical Profession* may remain ungeneralized.

This generalization option has been used in several articles such as those by Bayardo and Agrawal (2005), Fung et al. (2005), Fung et al. (2007), Iyengar (2002), and LeFevre et al. (2005).

6.2.1.3   Cell generalization

Generalization is performed on specific cells in the relation. Given several occurrences of a specific value in a relation, the value may be generalized in some of the occurrences, while in the others, it may remain ungeneralized. Generalizing a value in a specific cell does not lead to the generalization of other values in the relation. Because generalization can be limited to specific cells, generalization at the cell level is considered to be more flexible than the generalization schemes described earlier, resulting in a data release which has more specific values while still being considered as maintaining privacy. This generalization option has been used in several articles, for example, those of LeFevre et al. (2005), Wong et al. (2006), and Xu et al. (2006).

6.2.1.4   Multidimensional generalization

Given a relation that contains several attributes and taxonomy trees related to these attributes, a multidimensional generalization can be obtained by applying to the relation a single function which generalizes $qid=<v_1,..,v_n>$ to $qid'=<u_1,..,u_n>$, where for every v_i, either $v_i=u_i$ or v_i is a descendent node of u_i in the taxonomy of attribute i. This generalization option has been used in several articles, for example in [LeFevre, 2006].

The following several issues concerning generalizations are worth mentioning:

- It is common to represent generalized values of a continuous attribute (for example, salary and birth date) by intervals (taxonomy trees are not used for generalization of continuous attributes).
- There are cases of generalization without a predetermined hierarchal structure. The generalizations in [Yao, 2005] are outcomes of selection queries applied to a relation.
- Common considerations in selecting a specific anonymization scheme to be performed on a data release are:

  ○ The complexity of the overall anonymization process or algorithm used to find an anonymous table.
  ○ The amount of distortion created by the anonymization.

Generalization algorithms based on full-domain generalization schemes have the least complexity, but the largest amount of distortion, while generalization algorithms based on a cell generalization scheme have greater complexity, but less distortion.

6.2.2   Suppression

Data suppression is often used in conjunction with generalization and involves the omission of data. It may be thought of as a special case of generalization: a value is considered to be suppressed if it is generalized to the most general value in the domain. For example, assume that a set of database tuples have profession field values of *Doctor* and *Singer*. The minimal generalized value that can generalize all these specific values is the entire set * (according to Figure 6.1). These specific values are considered to be suppressed. Several suppression options are:

Tuple suppression: suppresses an entire row/tuple (used in several papers, for example [Bayardo, 2005]; [Iyengar, 2002]).

Attribute suppression: suppression is performed at the column level, obscuring all the values in a column (used, for example, in [Wang, 2005]).

Cell suppression (CS): suppression is performed at the individual cell level. As a result, an anonymized table may have data removed from certain cells of a given tuple or attribute (used in several articles, for example [Meyerson, 2004]).

6.2.3   Permutation

Permutation was proposed by Zhang et al. (2007). Assuming a table which includes sensitive and identifying attributes, they proposed to permute the projection of the table which consists of the sensitive attributes. In this way, the links between the identifying and sensitive attributes are destroyed, privacy is preserved, and the aggregation properties of the table are preserved as well.

6.2.4   Perturbation

Data perturbation refers to the replacement of the original values of the table with synthetic values. The synthetic values are chosen in such a way that statistical analyses performed on the table before and after replacement should not differ significantly.

Compared to other methods, data perturbation easily maintains anonymity (the data are not genuine); however, the published data are not reliable and consequently may not be useful. In contrast, generalization methods result in less precise, yet more reliable data.

Given the fact that only the statistical analysis that was used to guide the replacement of the values remains useful and similar to the original version, it is reasonable for the data publisher to publish the statistical information or the data mining results rather than the perturbed data [Domingo-Ferrer, 2008].

6.3   Privacy models

Several models have been developed to protect the privacy of individuals when publishing information related to them. All the models evolved from the first basic model k-anonymity.

6.3.1   Basic concepts

The following paragraphs describe some basic concepts which should provide a better understanding of the models which will be detailed later. Information about individuals contains several types of attributes. Attributes which describe an individual can be divided into several categories:

Identifiers (ID): These types of attributes uniquely identify the person. Typical examples include social security number and driver's license ID number.

Quasi-identifiers (QID): This category consists of attributes that do not provide a unique identification, but which in combination might yield a unique identification by means of linking attacks. For example, if the following tuple exists in a public table containing medical information: "male, age = 39, zip code = 636363, divorced, flu", and it is known that there is only one 39-years-old divorced male with zip code 636363, his medical status can be reveal.

Sensitive: These are attributes that contain private information about individuals such as their health, salary, and purchasing habits.

Non-sensitive: These attributes neither identify a person nor relate to sensitive private information about him or her.

6.3.2   k-Anonymity

The k-anonymity model [Sweeny, 2002a-b] assumes that a data owner wishes to publish a table that contains information about individuals. The information contains sensitive and descriptive data like age, gender, and birth date. To protect the privacy of individuals, attributes that uniquely identify them are not considered for publication.

It is also assumed that there might be an external source of information containing descriptive data together with identifiable data about specific individuals. If such an external source of information does exist, then by linking the information from the external source with the information from the data owner's table, a connection between the identifier and sensitive information might be established, and the privacy of the individuals might be violated.

Fig. 6.2 Compromising
privacy with QIDs

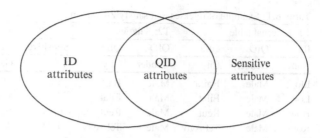

Sweeny cites an instance in which medical data about certain individuals were released by a data owner who believed that the data were anonymous. Sweeny purchased a voter registration list (which represents the external source of information) from the same area as the released medical data and linked the information from the two sources. As a consequence, medical information about these specific individuals was revealed and their privacy violated.

The linkage between the data holder's table and the external table was possible based on common attributes of the two sources of information. Sweeny claimed that the data holder should be expected to identify all attributes in the private information table that could possibly be used to link to external information and, moreover, that the set of such attributes constitutes a quasi-identifier.

Figure 6.2 illustrates the data owner's table. The right side of the oval contains quasi-identifier and sensitive attributes and the external source of information for each. On the left are identifier and quasi-identifier attributes.

The goal of Sweeny's work was to release person-specific data in such a way that the ability to link these data to other information using a quasi-identifier would be limited. Therefore, before publishing the data holder's table, there is a need to define which attributes will serve as QIDs and to adjust the table to adhere to k-anonymity. A table that adheres to k-anonymity is a table where each set of values in the table that is associated with a QID appears in the same table at least k times (see the formal definition below).

As a result of transforming the original table to adhere to k-anonymity, each tuple in the published table is indistinguishable from at least k-1 more tuples with respect to the values associated with the quasi-identifier attributes.

When trying to link the published table with an external table (which contains identifiers and quasi-identifiers), each tuple in the external table will be linked to at least k tuples of the published table (because each combination of values of a quasi-identifier attributes in the table is repeated at least k times). Consequently, the probability of linking an individual to a specific tuple through a QID is at most $1/k$.

As mentioned earlier, generalization and suppression are common techniques used to achieve k-anonymity. The following example describes the anonymization process (see Table 6.1). T1 is a possible published external source table which contains the ID and QID attributes *Name*, *Gender*, and *City*. T2 is the new table that needs to be published and which contains a sensitive attribute, *Salary*. T2* is the result of transforming T2 to adhere to k-anonymity, where $k=2$.

Table 6.1 Example of releases that satisfy 2-anonymity

T1: External table			T2: Salaries			T2*: 2-Anonymized table		
ID	QID	QID	QID	QID	Sensitive	QID	QID	Sensitive
Name	Gender	City	Gender	City	Salary	Gender	City	Salary
Ido	Male	Haifa	Male	Haifa	5000	Male	any	5000
Loly	Male	Eilat	Male	Eilat	5001	Male	any	5001
Bony	Male	Reut	Male	Reut	6000	Male	any	6000
Koby	Male	Tel Aviv	Male	Tel Aviv	4000	Any	Tel Aviv	4000
Kelly	Female	Tel Aviv	Female	Tel Aviv	10000	Any	Tel Aviv	10000

From T1 and T2, it is possible to infer that Ido earns 5000 NIS (Ido is the only male who lives in Haifa). From T1 and T2*, it cannot be known whether Ido's salary is 5000, 5001, or 6000.

6.3.2.1 A formal definition of *k*-anonymity

Let $RT(A_1,...,A_n)$ be a table, and let QID_{RT} be the quasi-identifier associated with it. RT is said to satisfy *k*-anonymity if and only if each sequence of values in $RT[QI_{RT}]$ appears with at least *k* occurrences in $RT[QID_{RT}]$.

6.3.3   L-Diversity

A major drawback of the *k*-anonymity model is that it does not enforce any diversity on the values of sensitive attributes. For example, assume a set of tuples which belong to the same *QID* group and which all have the same value of the sensitive attribute. Clearly, the individuals that correspond to these tuples cannot be distinguished from one another because they all have the same *QID*. However, the sensitive value for these individuals can be deduced easily because it is the same value for all.

The *l*-diversity model [Machanavajjhala, 2007] requires each *QID* group to contain at least *l* "well-represented" sensitive values.

Here, three instantiations of *l*-diversity are presented that differ in the manner in which "well-represented" is defined:

Entropy *l*-diversity: A table is *entropy l-diverse* if for each *QID* group,

$$-\sum_{s \in S} P(QID,S) \times \log(P(QID,S)) \geq \log(l)$$

where *S* is a sensitive attribute and *P(QID,S)* is the percentage of tuples within the *QID* group that contain the sensitive value *S*. The more evenly the sensitive values are distributed within a *QID* group, the higher the entropy value will be.

Table 6.2 A diversity
problem example

QID	QID	QID	Sensitive
Gender	Profession	Age	Problem
Male	Engineer	30	HIV
Male	Engineer	30	HIV
Male	Engineer	30	Flu
Female	Doctor	34	Obesity
Female	Doctor	34	Obesity
Female	Doctor	34	Flu
Female	Doctor	34	Flu

Therefore, a high l-threshold value implies less certainty of inferring a particular sensitive value in a QID group.

Recursive (c,l)-diversity: A table is *recursive (c,l)-diverse* if for each QID group, $r_1 < c(r_l + r_{l+1} + ... + r_m)$, where r_i denote the number of times that the ith most frequent sensitive value appears in the QID group, c is a constant, and m is the number of sensitive values in the QID group. This definition verifies that the most frequent value does not appear too frequently and that the less frequent values do not appear too rarely.

"Simple" l-diversity: A table is *l-diverse* if for each QID group and for each sensitive value S $P(QID,S) \leq 1/l$, where $P(QID,S)$ is the percentage of tuples within the QID group that contain the sensitive value S.

In the example below, as seen in Table 6.2, the entropy l-diversity instantiation is used. The QID groups are listed in the table and their entropy calculated according to the formula.

(1) "Male, Engineer, 30" appears three times in the table, once with the sensitive value *Flu* and twice with the sensitive value *HIV*. The entropy calculation is therefore:

$$-1/3^* log(1/3) - 2/3^* log(2/3) = log(1.89)$$

(2) "Female, Doctor, 34" appears four times in the table, twice with the sensitive value *Flu* and twice with the sensitive value *Obesity*. The entropy calculation is therefore:

$$-1/2^* log(1/2) - 1/2^* log(1/2) = log(2)$$

Therefore, the table satisfies entropy l-diversity if $l \leq 1.89$.

6.3.4 K-Uncertainty

In [Yao, 2005], the proposed anonymity model is based on the association between a value of an identifier attribute and that of a sensitive attribute. According to this model, anonymity is preserved if each value of an identifier attribute is associated

Table 6.3 Example of releases that satisfy 2-uncertainty

T1: External table		T2: Diseases release		
ID	QID	QID	QID	Sensitive
Name	Profession	Profession	Gender	Problem
Lili	Engineer	Engineer	Male	HIV
Bob	Engineer	Engineer	Female	Obesity

with at least *k* distinct values of a sensitive attribute, where *k* is a pre-determined integer.

Although in Yao's original paper this model was referred to as *k*-anonymity, it later received the name *k-uncertainty* [Gritzalis, 2008]. This model, in contrast to the *l*-diversity model, relates to a linkage between an identifier and certain sensitive attributes (instead of a linkage between a quasi-identifier and sensitive attributes) and is used in multiple-release publishing scenarios where the association (between the identifier and the sensitive values) is checked on the intersection of information of several releases.

The example in Table 6.3 illustrates the concept of *k*-uncertainty. The two releases adhere to 2- uncertainty (each identifier value is associated with two sensitive values).

6.3.5   (X,Y)-Privacy

The (*X,Y*)-*privacy* model [Wang, 2006] described in this section is more general than the previously described models (*k*-anonymity, *l*-diversity, and *k*-uncertainty). Similarly to *k*-uncertainty, (X,Y)-privacy enables the expression of multiple-publication scenarios. This model assumes that there are two disjoint groups of attributes, X and Y, which describe individuals and sensitive properties. A violation of privacy occurs when it becomes possible to link specific values of (X) to specific values of (Y). The (X,Y)-privacy model is composed of two submodels: (X,Y)-anonymity and (X,Y)-linkability (described below). In other words, to satisfy (X,Y)-privacy, the published data need to satisfy both (X,Y)-anonymity and (X,Y)-linkability.

6.3.6   (X,Y)-Anonymity

To break any possible linkage between X and Y, the (*X,Y*)-*anonymity* model requires that each value of X be linked to at least *k* distinct values of Y, where *k* is some pre-determined integer.

K-uncertainty can be considered as a special case of this model in which the *identifier* attribute is represented by X and the *sensitive* attribute is represented by Y.

It is worth mentioning that another option in which X represents a QID and Y represents the sensitive attribute is also possible.

6.3.6.1 A formal definition

Assume the following:

- Table T
- Table attributes denoted by att(T)
- Number of tuples in the table is denoted by $|T|$
- $X, Y \subseteq att(T)$ and $X \cap Y = \emptyset$
- $\pi(T), \sigma(T)$ represent projection and selection over T respectively
- $|\pi_Y \sigma_x(T)|$ is the number of distinct values on Y that are related to $x (\in X)$
- $\min K = \min_{x \in X} |\pi_Y \sigma_x(T)|$ (min K is referred also as $A_Y(X)$)

(X,Y)-anonymity is violated if $\min K < k$ (where k is a specified integer threshold).

6.3.7 (X,Y)-Linkability

To break any possible linkage between X and Y, the *(X,Y)-linkability* model requires that the probability of inferring a specific value of Y, given a specific value of X, must be less than p (a predetermined threshold fraction) for all values in the table.

Consider the published tables 6.4(T1) and 6.4(T2). X is a QID (profession) and Y is the sensitive attribute (problem). Although the published table adheres to (X,Y)-anonymity, where $k=3$, (i.e., each profession is linked to at least three different problems), the probability of deducing which problem each engineer has is greater than one-third. For instance, the probability that an engineer suffers from HIV is two-thirds (there are six records with an "engineer" value, of which four contain the sensitive value *HIV*).

Table 6.4 Linkability problem example

T1: External table		T2: Disease release	
ID	QID	QID	Sensitive
Name	Profession	Profession	Problem
Lili	Engineer	Engineer	HIV
Bob	Engineer	Engineer	HIV
Ron	Engineer	Engineer	HIV
Loona	Engineer	Engineer	HIV
Eve	Engineer	Engineer	Obesity
Nimrod	Engineer	Engineer	Flu
Lili	Engineer	Engineer	HIV

6.3.7.1   A formal definition

Assume:

- Table T
- Table attributes denoted by att(T)
- Number of tuples in the table is denoted by |T|
- $X,Y \subseteq att(T)$ and $X \cap Y = \emptyset$
- $\sigma(T)$ denotes selection over T
- $|\sigma_x(T)|$ is the number of tuples in T containing x ($\in X$)
- $|\sigma_{x,y}(T)|$ is the number of tuples in T containing both x ($\in X$) and y ($\in Y$)
- $link(x,y) = |\sigma_{x,y}(T)| / |\sigma_x(T)|$
- $\max\ link = \max_{x \in X, y \in Y} link(x,y)$ (max Link is referred also as $L_Y(X)$)

(X,Y)-linkability is violated if maxLink > p (where p is a pre-determined real threshold).

6.4   Metrics

6.4.1   Information metrics

To satisfy a given anonymity model, the published data might be anonymized. As a consequence of the anonymization process, the quality and utility of the data will likely deteriorate.

This section focuses on information metrics used to measure data quality and utility. It is worth mentioning that measures of data quality might depend on the data recipient's information needs. An information metric which is good for one recipient may not be as highly regarded by another recipient. This section elaborates on general information metrics that are not oriented to a request for specific data by a recipient.

The most intuitive information metric is to measure the resemblance between the original data and the anonymous data. In this metric, each value that is different in the anonymized table from the corresponding value in the original table is assigned a value of one.

In the minimal-distortion or MD metric [Samarati, 2001]; [Sweeney, 1997]; [Wang, 2006], a penalty is charged for each generalized value v_g: $MD(V_g) = H(V_g)$, where $H(v_g)$ is the height of v_g in the generalization tree. For example, generalizing one instance of *Doctor* to *Medical Profession* in Figure 6.1 results in MD(*Medical Profession*) = 1.

A more sophisticated metric is ILoss, which was proposed in [Iyengar, 2002]. ILoss associates each table cell with a number between 0 (no generalization at all) and 1 (total suppression) which is proportional to the size of the generalized subset in that cell. The following equation represents this concept:

$$ILOSS(V_g) = \frac{|V_g| - 1}{|D_A| - 1}$$

where $|V_g|$ is the number of leaf descendants of v_g and $|D_A|$ is the number of domain values for attribute A. It is possible to add weights to the generalized attributes to reflect their importance. It is also possible to normalize the result of the information loss in a specific release to be between 0 and 1 by dividing the sum of the information loss of all cells in the release by the dimensions of the release.

In contrast to previously mentioned metrics, in which each value in a release is measured independently of the other values in a release, in the discernibility metric (DM) [Bayardo, 2005], the penalty charged for each value depends on other values in the release.

The DM charges a penalty for each tuple that is indistinguishable from other tuples with respect to a QID. If a tuple belongs to a group of size s, the penalty for the tuple will be s. This metric is exactly the opposite of k-anonymization, which seeks to make tuples indistinguishable with respect to a QID. This metric is used in [Machanavajjhala, 2006], [Xu, 2006], and [LeFerve, 2006].

The cost of generalization based on entropy computation is a classical measure used in information theory to characterize the purity of data. Entropy has been used in [Sweeney, 1997], [Goldberg, 2010], and [Gionis, 2009] to measure information loss.

6.4.2 Search metrics

To transform a basic table into an anonymized table, an anonymization algorithm is generally applied to the basic table.

A search metric guides each step of the anonymization (search) algorithm to identify an anonymous table with maximum information or minimum distortion.

This is frequently achieved by ranking a set of possible anonymization operations to be applied to the table using a search metric and then greedily performing the "best" operation at each step in the search. Several examples of search metrics are described below.

Distinctive attribute (DA): This metric, presented by Sweeny (1997), was used to guide the search for an attribute to be generalized. The attribute selected was the one which had the greatest number of distinctive values in the data presented for generalization.

Information versus privacy tradeoff: This metric was presented by Fung et al. (2008). The premise of tradeoff metrics is to consider both the privacy and information requirements of each anonymization operation and eventually to select and perform the operation that best fits these two constraints.

Later in this book the use of the tradeoff metric in specialization and generalization operations is demonstrated.

Specialization: A table is generalized to the most general values and then iteratively specialized. In each specialization operation, additional information is revealed. Consequently, some new information may be gained, but there may also be a loss of privacy (of the entities represented in the table).

In the following equation, $IG(s)$ refers to the amount of information gained, while $PL(s)$ refers to the amount of privacy lost from applying the specialization operation s:

$$IGPL(s) = IG(s) / (PL(s) + 1)$$

IG can be measured, for example, by decreasing the value associated with the MD metric presented above or by using the entropy formula. PL can be measured, for example, by a decrease in the privacy threshold that the table maintains. For instance, if the privacy model is k-anonymity and if before specialization the table satisfies 100-anonymity and after specialization the table satisfies 97-anonymity, then the value of PL will be 3.

Generalization: A table is iteratively generalized until a privacy model is satisfied. In each generalization operation, information is omitted, and therefore some information content is lost. However, at the same time, privacy (of the entities represented in the table) might be gained.

In the following equation, $IL(s)$ refers to the amount of information lost and $PG(s)$ to the amount of privacy gained from applying the generalization operation g: $ILPG(s) = IL(s)/(PG(s) + 1)$.

6.5 Standard anonymization algorithms

This section elaborates on anonymization algorithms based on generalization and suppression operations. Each algorithm is designed to adjust a table before publication to prevent a particular privacy model from being violated. In the first part of this section, two techniques for anonymizing a table are introduced.

Bottom-Up Generalization
With this technique, the algorithm takes the original data that may violate the anonymity model (for example, k-anonymity) and iteratively generalizes them until the data satisfy the anonymity model.

Top-Down Specialization
With this technique, the algorithm generalizes all values in the table to the most general values according to a specified taxonomy tree. The algorithm then iteratively specializes the values until no specialization can be performed without violating the anonymity model that has been selected.

The second part of this section distinguishes between anonymization algorithms according to the following two broad categories: optimal anonymization and greedy anonymization.

Optimal Anonymization

Each algorithm in this category finds an optimal anonymization (for a specific privacy model) for a given data metric. Finding an optimal solution requires an exhaustive search that may not be scalable. Because of this possibility, the algorithms are first applied to a small dataset, using full-domain generalization and tuple suppression. These operations reduce the search space compared to other generalization operations such as cell generalization.

Many algorithms for producing optimal k-anonymous tables through attribute generalization and tuple suppression have been proposed, as described following.

Sweeney (2002b) proposed an algorithm that exhaustively examines all potential generalization options and identified the one that minimally satisfies k-anonymity.

LeFevre et al. (2005) proposed an optimal algorithm, Incognito, which uses a bottom-up technique with *a priori* computation. The algorithm calculates the parent group size (group size of the QID) from the sum of all child group sizes. Use of this technique provides a termination condition for the search for generalization options (in the case where all group sizes are at least K, then there is no need to generalize the table further).

These algorithms find exact solutions for the k-anonymity problem. Other algorithms exist that also find optimal solutions with reference to a different privacy model, such as the algorithm presented by [Machanavajjhala, 2006] that modifies the bottom-up algorithm proposed by [LeFevre, 2005] to create an optimal l-diverse table.

Greedy Anonymization

Each algorithm in this category finds a local "greedy" anonymization table. In each step of the anonymization process, all candidate generalization or specialization operations are ranked according to a search metric. The best candidate is chosen, and the generalization or specialization operation is executed on the table. Algorithms in the greedy anonymization category are more scalable for large datasets and for various generalization techniques (including cell and cut/subtree generalization) than optimal anonymization.

The following paragraphs present several algorithms for producing greedily anonymous tables (according to a privacy model).

Hundepool and Willenborg (1996) presented an algorithm that greedily applies subtree generalizations and cell suppressions to achieve k-anonymity.

This method computes the frequency of all possible combinations of values of three attributes and performs generalization accordingly. The resulting data may not be k-anonymous when more than three attributes are considered.

Sweeney (1997) presented the first scalable algorithm (called Datafly) that handles large data sets. It produces a k-anonymous solution by generating an array of QID group sizes and then greedily generalizes those combinations with fewer than k occurrences according to a heuristic search metric that chooses the attribute with the largest number of distinct values. Datafly uses full-domain generalization and tuple suppression.

Iyengar (2002) proposed an algorithm based on genetic algorithms and solves the k-anonymity problem using an incomplete stochastic search method which implements a classification metric as a search metric.

Wang et al. (2004) presented a bottom-up generalization algorithm based on the ILPG search metric previously discussed.

Fung et al. (2008) presented a top-down specialization algorithm based on the ILPG search metric.

LeFevre et al. (2006) proposed a greedy top-down specialization algorithm (Mondrian Multidimensional) that generates a greedy k-anonymization table for the case of the multidimensional generalization option.

Gionis et al. (2008) proposed a set of agglomerative clustering algorithms. These algorithms depend on a definition of a distance function between subsets of tuples. The basic agglomerative k-anonymization algorithm proposed in this paper starts with a set of singleton clusters, where each cluster represents a tuple in the original table. The algorithm operates iteratively; in each iteration, it unifies the two closest clusters (having the minimal distance between them). The clusters are unified until they mature into clusters of size at least k (the modified agglomerative k-anonymization algorithm takes clusters size into account to avoid clusters significantly larger than k). It is worth mentioning that Nergiz and Clifton (2006) also described an agglomerative algorithm.

Goldberger and Tassa (2010) proposed a sequential clustering algorithm related to the k-anonymity privacy model. This algorithm starts with a random partition of the tuples into clusters. Then, it reviews all tuples in a cyclic manner and checks for each tuple whether it could be transferred from its current cluster into another one, thereby increasing the utility of the anonymization. This algorithm iterates until either a local optimum is reached (i.e., a state in which no single-tuple transition offers an improvement) or local improvements in utility become very small.

It is worth mentioning that this article presents an extension to an algorithm that also supports the l-diversity privacy model. This algorithm was compared (in an experimental evaluation) with four well-known algorithms for k-anonymity and achieved the best utility results.

Because these approaches are heuristic algorithms, no bounds on the efficiency and quality of the solutions can be given. However, experimental results can be used to assess the quality of the solutions generated by these approaches.

6.6   Multiple-release publishing

Real-life applications include scenarios in which a data owner may wish to publish several releases that contain information about a certain population [Shmueli, 2012]. Below are several examples of such scenarios:

- Information requirements are not known in advance, but are added over a period of time.
- New information about the population is collected over a period of time.
- Each release serves different needs or, for example, a different data mining purpose.
- The data being published are continuously being updated.

Table 6.5   Multiple releases and join table example

Release 1 (R1)			Release 2 (R2)			Join R1+R2		
X	X	Y (sensitive)	X	X	Y (sensitive)	X	X	Y (sensitive)
Profession	Gender	Problem	Profession	Gender	Problem	Profession	Gender	Problem
Doctor	*	Obesity	*	Male	Obesity	Doctor	Male	Obesity
Doctor	*	Flu	*	Female	Flu	Doctor	Female	Flu
Gardener	*	Cancer	*	Male	Cancer	Gardener	Male	Cancer
Gardener	*	Headache	*	Female	Headache	Gardener	Female	Headache

6.6.1   Single vs. multiple-release publishing

The anonymization process performed when multiple releases are published should differ from the process performed when a single release is published.

Consider the example provided in Table 6.5. Each release satisfies (X,Y)-anonymity when $k=2$. However, when joining (on the sensitive attribute) the information published in these two releases, it is apparent that each X-value refers to only one Y-(sensitive) value, thus violating (X,Y)-anonymity when $k=2$.

The anonymization process performed on a single new release in a single-release publishing scenario takes into account the single release to be published, while in a multiple-release publishing scenario, the anonymization process should consider the single release to be published and all previously published releases.

6.6.2   Publishing releases in parallel

This situation occurs when several releases are published at one time from a specific source of information.

Motivation

A relevant question that may arise before publishing a number of releases at a specific time is, *Why not publish a single release containing all the information from all the releases?* There might be several answers to this question. For example, there are very possibly several data recipients who are interested in different parts of the data (each recipient is interested in different attributes). Or maybe various data recipients are interested in the same data, but have different ideas regarding the importance of the specific data that are to be published (this could lead, for example, to a different anonymization algorithm). Below is an example to help illustrate the situation.

Consider a case in which a need or request has been expressed to publish the following two sources of information (two tables):

- A table containing the attributes: *age, gender, problem.*
- A table containing the attributes: *profession, gender, problem.*

By publishing a unified table that contains the attributes of age, profession, gender, and problem, a connection between the attribute's age and profession is established. The connection, which is neither needed nor requested, reveals information about the individuals represented in the table and thus possibly intrudes upon the privacy of the individuals covered by the data. Moreover, the data anonymized in the unified table may be less suitable to the two different needs or requests than publishing two releases. Nergiz et al. (2007) and Dwork (2006) have dealt with the scenario of parallel release publishing.

6.6.3 Publishing releases in sequence

This scenario may occur when information requirements are not known in advance or when new information is collected and added over a period of time. Publishing releases in parallel is a special case of publishing in sequence. Parallel release publishing may have an advantage over sequential publishing, which is based on knowledge of all information requirements in advance. This advantage could be used to balance the amount of information published in each release before publishing the releases.

The sequential release publishing scenario is probably the most interesting scenario. Two naïve solutions exist for this type of scenario [Samarati, 1998]; [Sweeney 2002a]: (1) anonymize the underlying table once and then publish releases based on the anonymized table, and (2) generalize each new release based on previous releases in such a manner that each value in the new release is no more specific than the same value published in previous releases. However, both these solutions suffer from a higher degree of data distortion than is necessary.

The following subsections describe in detail two well-known studies: "Anonymizing sequential releases" [Wang, 2006] and "Checking for k-anonymity violation by views" [Yao, 2005].

6.6.4 Anonymizing sequential releases

In [Wang, 2006], a formalized definition for anonymizing sequential releases was given, and a top-down specialization algorithm for anonymizing sequential releases (TDS4ASR) was proposed.

The sequential anonymization problem can be defined as follows. A data holder owns a private base table T. The data holder has divided several attributes in T into two groups, X and Y, which describe individuals and their sensitive properties. The data holder has previously released a table T_2 and wants to release the next table T_1, where T_2 and T_1 are projections of the same underlying table T and contain some common attributes. The data holder wants to ensure (X,Y)-privacy on the match join of T_1 and T_2 (the join concept used in TDS4ASR is also referred to by the term *match join*). To ensure (X,Y)-privacy, T_1 must be generalized on the attributes $X \cap \mathrm{att}(T_1)$ (according to the cut generalization model) while keeping the data as useful as possible.

The TDS4ASR algorithm uses a top-down approach in which all values in the table associated with the $X \cap \mathrm{att}(T_1)$ attributes are generalized to the most general value (ANY) according to a specified taxonomy tree defined for each attribute and are iteratively specialized until no specialization can be performed without violating (X,Y)-privacy. An important justification for choosing this approach is based on the anti-monotonicity property of (X,Y)-privacy with respect to specialization, which states that if (X,Y)-privacy has been violated, it remains violated after a specialization operation. Two proofs are given in the article for the antimonotonicity property:

- Given T_1 and T_2, $A_Y(X)$ does not increase after a specialization of T_1 on $X \cap \mathrm{att}(T_1)$.
- If Y contains attributes from T_1 or T_2, but not from both, $L_Y(X)$ does not decrease after a specialization of T_1 on the attributes $X \cap \mathrm{att}(T_1)$.

As a result of this property additional specializations can be stopped whenever (X,Y)-privacy is violated for the first time.

Following is a more detailed description of the TDS4ASR algorithm. As mentioned earlier, the TDS4ASR algorithm generalizes $X \cap \mathrm{att}(T_1)$ attributes of T_1 according to the cut generalization scheme to satisfy the given (X,Y)-privacy on the match-join (the match join algorithm is shown below) of T_1 and T_2. The algorithm operates iteratively. At first, each attribute A_j in the common attributes of X and T_1 (denoted by X_1) is generalized to the most general value, ANY_j. In the following iterations, all valid candidates for specialization are found. A valid candidate is a candidate that does not violate the privacy requirement after its specialization. The candidate with the highest score (according to a specified heuristic) is specialized. The process ends when no more candidates can be found. The TDS4ASR algorithm is shown below an Algorithm 6.1.

Algorithm 6.1 Top-Down Specialization for Anonymizing Sequential Releases (TDS4ASR)

Input: T_1, T_2, an (X,Y)-privacy requirement, a taxonomy tree for each category attribute in X_1.

Output: a generalized T_1 satisfying the privacy requirement.

01: generalize every value of A_j to ANY_j where $A_j \in X_1$;
02: **while** there is a valid candidate in $\cup$ *Cutj* **do**
03: find the winner w of the highest $Score(w)$ from $\cup$ *Cutj* ;
04: specialize w on T_1 and remove w from $\cap$ *Cutj* ;
05: add all child values of w according to the taxonomy tree to $\cap$ *Cutj* ;
06: update $Score(v)$ and the valid status for all v in $\cap$ *Cutj* ;
07: **end while**
08: output the generalized T_1 and $\cap Cutj$;

Remarks:

- *Cutj* contains the current generalized values of attribute A_j.
- A valid candidate is a value for which the privacy requirement is not violated in the match-join table of T_1 and T_2 after its specialization.
- Each value is given a score according to some metric of information gain and privacy loss.

The match-join algorithm used by the TDS4ASR algorithm is shown in Algorithm 6.2. For each two tuples $t_1 \in T_1$ and $t_2 \in T_2$ that match, the match-join table J contains their concatenated tuple. Two tuples match if and only if for every common categorical attribute A: $t_1.A$ and $t_2.A$ are on the same generalization path in the taxonomy tree for A.

Algorithm 6.2 Match-Join
___

Input: T_1, T_2

Output: J, the match join table of T_1 and T_2

01: $J = \emptyset$
02: **for all** $t_1 \in T_1$;
03:      **for all** $t_2 \in T_2$;
04:            **if** match(t_1, t_2) **then**
05:                 $t =$ concatenate (t_1, t_2) ;
06:                 $J = J \cap \{t\}$
07:            **end if** ;
08:      **end** for ;
09: **end** for ;
10: **return** J ;
___

6.6.4.1 Checking for *k*-anonymity violation by views

[Yao, 2005] presented a method for detecting *k*-anonymity violation on a set of views, each view being obtained from a projection and selection query over a private base table containing an identifier attribute (ID) and a sensitive or private attribute (P). According to the method or algorithm for detecting *k*-anonymity violation, a violation of privacy occurs if a quasi-identifier (QID) value can be associated with fewer than *k* distinct sensitive or private (P) values. It is important to mention that the tuples presented in the view (returned by the query) are distinct, or in other words, that duplicate tuples are removed.

6.6.4.2 Privacy preserving data mining

Knowledge discovery in databases (KDD) is the process of identifying valid, novel, useful, and understandable patterns from large datasets. Data mining (DM) is the core of the KDD process and involves algorithms that explore the data, develop models, and discover significant patterns. Data mining has emerged as a key tool for a wide variety of applications ranging from national security to market analysis. Many of these applications involve mining data which include private and sensitive information about users.

To avoid such situations, privacy regulations have been promulgated in many countries (e.g., privacy regulations as part of HIPAA in the United States). The data owner is required to omit identifying data so as to ensure, with high probability, that private information about individuals cannot be inferred from the datasets that are released for analysis or sent to another data owner. At the same time, omitting important fields from datasets, such as age in a medical domain, might reduce the accuracy of the model that can be derived from the data by the DM process. *Privacy-preserving data mining* (*PPDM*) deals with the tradeoff between the effectiveness of the mining process and the privacy of the subjects, with the aim of minimizing privacy exposure with a minimal effect on mining results [Kisilevich, 2010].

Verykios et al. (2004) classified existing PPDM approaches based on five dimensions: (1) data distribution, referring to whether the data are centralized or distributed; (2) data modification, referring to the modifications performed on the data values to ensure privacy. Various possible operations such as aggregation (also called generalization) or swapping are included; (3) data mining algorithms, which refer to the target DM algorithm for which the PPDM method has been defined (e.g., classification); (4) data or rule hiding, which refers to whether the PPDM method hides the raw or the aggregated data; and finally, (5) privacy preservation, which refers to the type of technique used for privacy preservation: heuristic, cryptographic, or reconstruction-based (i.e., perturbing the data and reconstructing the distributions to perform mining).

One of the PPDM techniques uses the concept of *k*-anonymity described above. However, the systems mentioned earlier do not assume that any specific DM algorithm has been performed on the dataset. PPDM considers the anonymity problem in terms of mining, or in other words, operations are performed on the data while taking into account their effect on mining results. In particular, a few studies have addressed the use of *k*-anonymity for classification. In one study, a random genetic algorithm has been used to search for the optimal generalization of data [Iyengar, 2002]. This algorithm seems to be impractical because of its computational extensiveness. The author reported an 18-hour run for 30K records. Wang et al. (2004) presented a practical effective bottom-up generalization approach aimed at preserving the information needed to induce the classifier while preserving privacy. They defined the *information gain* metric to measure the privacy versus information tradeoff. The bottom-up generalization technique can generalize on categorical attributes only. Fung et al. (2007) presented another practical generalization method for classification using *k*-anonymity, the *top-down specialization* (*TDS*) algorithm. This algorithm can handle both categorical and continuous attributes. TDS starts from the most general state of the table and specializes it by assigning specific values to attributes until a violation of anonymity occurs. An improved version of TDS called *TDR* (*top-down refinement*) has been introduced [Fung, 2007]. In addition to the capabilities of TDS, TDR is capable of suppressing a categorical attribute with no taxonomy tree. It uses a single-dimension recoding approach, or in other words, an aggressive suppression operator that suppresses a certain value in all records without considering the values of other attributes, so that the data which might adhere to k-anonymity might also be suppressed. This *over-suppression* reduces the quality of the anonymous datasets.

Friedman et al. (2009) presented kADET, a decision-tree induction algorithm which is guaranteed to maintain k-anonymity. The main idea was to embed the k-anonymity constraint into the groining phase of a decision tree. Although kADET has shown accuracy superior to that of other methods, it is limited to decision-tree inducers. It differs from other methods like TDS and TDR by letting data owners share with each other the classification models extracted from their own private datasets, rather than letting the data owners publish any of their own private datasets. Therefore, the output of kADET is an anonymous decision tree rather than an anonymous dataset.

Sharkey et al. (2008) presented the APT algorithm which, like kADET, outputs an anonymous decision tree rather than an anonymous dataset. In addition, the authors showed how the classification model can then be used to generate a pseudo-dataset; however, the pseudo-dataset is tightly coupled to the classification model. Because the classifier is not an authentic anonymous copy of the original private dataset, neither is the pseudo-dataset. For example, the values of the non-quasi-identifier attributes (which can be shared with no risk) are lost if they are not included in the classification model. Similarly, the actual distribution of non-binary target attributes can be distorted (the number of tuples in each class is only roughly estimated).

Chapter 7
Case studies

This chapter presents three case studies in the data leakage domain and the methods proposed and evaluated for mitigating the threat of data leakage. The case studies are: detecting an insider attempting to misuse and leak data stored in a database system; using honeytokens to detect insider threats; and detecting leakage through email.

7.1   Misuse detection in database systems

Protecting sensitive tabular data (e.g., customer or medical records) from unauthorized disclosure is a major concern in every organization. Because the organization's employees and its business partners need access to such data to carry out their daily work, data leakage detection and prevention are both an essential and a challenging task. One of the great challenges is to identify suspicious access to database by insiders.

In this scenario, the assumption is that users interact with a system using a client application (e.g., a Web browser) and can submit requests (for data) to perform various tasks. Requests are submitted to an application server that interacts with a database to retrieve the required data and send the result sets to the user. Each user accesses the system within a specific role (e.g., a manager) and is assigned a set of permissions to allow him or her to perform tasks. This however, creates a problem, because a user may exploit his/her legitimate access rights to leak data or to take actions that are not in line with the organization's goals. Here, two methods aimed at detecting unauthorized tabular data disclosure by an insider will be presented.

A. Shabtai et al., *A Survey of Data Leakage Detection and Prevention Solutions*,
SpringerBriefs in Computer Science, DOI 10.1007/978-1-4614-2053-8_7,
© The Author(s) 2012

7.1.1 Applying unsupervised context-based analysis

As presented in Section 4.2.2, most research efforts in this domain have focused on deriving behavioral profiles that define normal user behavior and which issue an alert whenever a user's behavior deviates from the normal profile. A user profile can be generated using a syntax-centric approach [Karma, 2008] or a data-centric approach [Sunu, 2009].

The first method presented here describes a new unsupervised approach for identifying suspicious access to sensitive relational data. The proposed method creates links between entities using a *one-class clustering tree* (OCCT). A clustering tree is a tree in which each of the leaves contains a cluster instead of a single classification. Each cluster is generalized by a set of rules which is stored in the appropriate leaf. The goal of using the OCCT in this domain is to derive a model that encapsulates the characteristics of the result-set (i.e., data) that the user normally accesses within each possible context. Thus, the OCCT links a set of records representing the context of the request (i.e., actual accesses to certain data) with a set of records representing the data which can be legitimately retrieved within the specific context. Thus, the inner nodes of the OCCT represent the contextual attributes within which the request occurs and the set of rules in the leaves represents the data which can be legitimately retrieved within the specific context. The rules are extracted using frequent item sets and define what data may be viewed within the specific context with which the leaf is associated.

The training set, which is used for generating the detection model, is composed of result sets and the context in which they were retrieved. The requests in the training set do not need to be labeled (under the assumption that most of the log records are legitimate), and therefore learning is unsupervised.

During the detection phase, the appropriate set of rules is obtained according to the context of the request. A record in the result-set that matches at least one of the rules is considered to be normal. The result set's score is the proportion of its records which are marked as normal. If the result-set achieves a similarity score greater than a predefined threshold, the action is considered to be legitimate. By analyzing both the context of the request and the data to which the user is exposed (i.e., the result-set), the method enhances detection accuracy and better distinguishes between normal and abnormal requests. This is important because the same request may be legitimate if performed within one context, but abnormal within another context.

7.1.1.1 Induction of the detection model

A detection model is a one-class clustering tree in which each leaf in the tree represents a cluster of records that can be accessed legitimately within the specific context (Figure 7.1). The characteristics of the cluster are represented by a set of rules (e.g., frequent item sets). Therefore, inducing the detection model is a two-step process: (1) constructing the detection model; (2) generating the leaf rule sets.

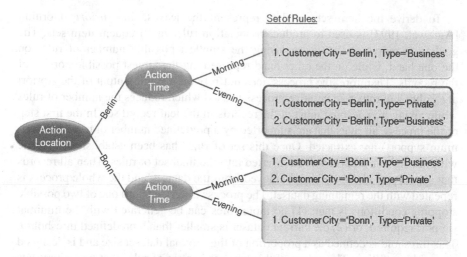

Set of Rules:

1. Customer City = 'Berlin', Type='Business'

1. Customer City = 'Berlin', Type='Private'
2. Customer City = 'Berlin', Type='Business'

1. Customer City = 'Bonn', Type='Business'
2. Customer City = 'Bonn', Type='Private'

1. Customer City = 'Bonn', Type='Private'

Fig. 7.1 Example of a one-class clustering tree detection model

The construction of the decision tree is an iterative process. In each step, a context attribute is selected as the next splitting attribute, and the node dataset is split
into smaller datasets according to the values of the splitting attribute. Similarly to
existing measures (e.g., entropy), a measure that ranks the context attributes has
been defined. The rankings are based on the attribute's ability to distinguish between
the subsets of each of the possible values of the attribute. To choose the next attribute for splitting, the *Jaccard similarity coefficient* [Guha, 2000] is calculated for
each possible split (i.e., the intersection of all complete records, divided by the
union size). If the examined attribute has more than two possible values, each possible value is examined against the union of all other subsets. The final score for the
attribute is calculated as the weighted average of all the calculated outcomes. The
weight of each score is determined by the ratio of the size of the subset and the size
of the record set before the current split. This approach is proposed instead of that
of examining each possible pair of subsets because the authors expect that the second method will yield very low similarity scores and will therefore be less
accurate.

Once the tree model has been induced, each leaf will contain a subset of records
that are normally retrieved within the specific context defined by the path that starts
from the root node and ends at the leaf node. At this stage, each subset of records is
represented as a set of rules determined by finding frequent item sets [Agrawal,
1993] that best describe the leaf dataset. These frequent item sets will be referred to
as *rules*. The rules are derived from the sensitive attributes and the context attributes
which were not chosen as splitting attributes during the construction of the tree. In
the detection phase, a record in the result set that matches at least one of the rules is
considered normal; otherwise, it is marked as abnormal. For example, according to
the highlighted leaf in Figure 7.1, transactions which are performed in Berlin in the
evening usually retrieve private or business customer records from Berlin.

To derive the item sets used to represent the leaves, the *Apriori* algorithm [Agrawal, 1993] is used to produce association rules and frequent item sets. The goal is to represent the dataset using the smallest possible number of rules on the one hand, while on the other hand representing the largest possible portion of the records. Therefore, the process does not rely on a single output of the Apriori algorithm, but rather an iterative process is used which reduces the number of rules while taking into account most of the records in the leaf record set. In the first step of the process, all rules that are supported by a predefined number of records (minimum support) are extracted. Once this set of rules has been established, the rule with the highest support will be inserted into the final set of rules. Then all records that support the chosen rule are removed from the dataset, and the whole process is repeated with the remaining dataset. The process is iterated until one of two possible stopping conditions is met: (1) no more rules can be generated with the minimal support required; or (2) the current dataset is smaller than a predefined threshold t. This threshold is defined as a proportion of the original dataset size and is designed to avoid overfitting. The output of this process is a set of rules that best represents the dataset matching the specific leaf.

There are two advantages of representing the leaves as a set of rules rather than keeping the legitimate set of data in each of the leaves. First, this makes it possible to create a smaller and more generalized representation of the data. In addition, this approach can better accommodate frequent changes in the database. When the entire dataset is kept in a leaf, any change in the database (e.g., INSERT, DELETE) might result in an outdated dataset. This would mean that retraining would be needed often. However, if the leaf dataset were represented as a set of rules, changes in the database would not necessarily require retraining.

7.1.1.2   Preliminary evaluation

Because no real dataset was available for evaluation, the authors chose to generate a simulated dataset. The simulated data were generated according to real scenarios described in [Gafny, 2010]. The data include requests for customer records of an organization submitted by a business partner of the organization. Contextual information on the requests includes the time of execution, day of execution, geographical location of the action, the user's role, and the type of action. Sensitive customer information includes each customer's name, address, zip code, place of work, and customer type (e.g., business, private, or student).

The simulated requests were generated according to one of the following three behavior types: (1) *Normal* behavior (retrieving customer records within the same geographical location during store opening hours); (2) *Malicious1* (retrieving the record of a customer who is not in the same geographical location as the store during opening hours); and (3) *Malicious2* behavior (searching for any customer record after closing time).

In addition, two types of users were defined: a *benign user* who submits legitimate requests most of the time, but who, on rare occasions, might have to perform actions that may seem malicious, but are actually required in the course of his work.

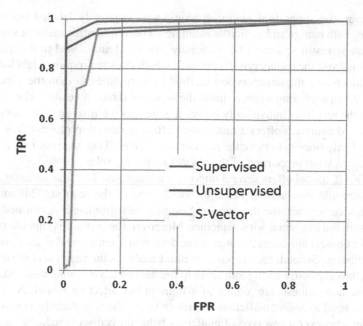

Fig. 7.2 ROC curves of the supervised [Gafny, 2010], S-vector [Sunu, 2009] and unsupervised OCCT models

A *malicious user* is an employee who queries the database for a purpose other than his work (e.g., data harvesting). The authors believe that a malicious user might try to hide his malicious intentions by mixing malicious queries with legitimate ones.

The goal of the evaluation process presented here was identify correctly as many malicious transactions (true positive) as possible while keeping false alarms (false positive) to a minimum.

The evaluation results are presented in the ROC graph shown in Figure 7.2. When the threshold is set to 0.5 (an anomaly score greater than this would imply that the request may be malicious), the algorithm yields a high true positive rate (TPR) of 0.93 with a false positive rate (FPR) of 0.09. When the threshold is set to 0.55, the TPR is slightly reduced to 0.88, but the FPR is reduced to 0.01. The proposed solution was also compared with the supervised solution presented in [Gafny, 2010]. In addition, the S-vector method [Sunu, 2009] was extended to take context into account by clustering the requests according to various context attributes and creating an S-vector for each context.

Figure 7.2 presents the ROC curves of the proposed unsupervised method, the supervised algorithm presented in [Gafny, 2010], and the best setting of the S-vector approach (achieved by setting the city and the request type as the context attributes). It is apparent that the supervised approach yields slightly better results than the unsupervised approach. In addition, using the area under the curve (AUC) measure, the supervised approach yields the highest score (0.9906), followed by the unsupervised approach (0.9627). The S-vector approach yields an AUC of 0.9346.

However, the supervised approach requires a completely labeled training set containing both benign and malicious examples. This implies that malicious requests and matching result sets must be artificially generated and added to the database. This differs from the unsupervised approach which does not require a labeled training set. Moreover, the unsupervised method is more efficient than the supervised method. When analyzing a new request, the supervised model needs to classify each record in the result set individually before it generates the final anomaly score. The unsupervised approach offers a much more efficient detection process. The model is scanned only once to retrieve the relevant set of rules. Then the result set is examined to assess what proportion of the records match the rules.

The OCCT model offers several important advantages. The first advantage is the ability to profile user actions based on the context of the request. This improves detection accuracy because the same request may be legitimate if performed within one context, but abnormal within another. Moreover, the method is capable of identifying the context attributes that maximize detection accuracy and considering only these attributes. Second, the proposed method analyzes the result sets retrieved by the user, thus explicitly taking into account the data which might be misused. Third, only legitimate requests are required for training the detection model. As a result, there is no need to collect malicious records or to add them artificially, nor to retrain the model whenever a new type of malicious behavior is discovered.

7.1.2   Calculating a misusability score for tabular data

In the academic research review in Section 4.2, it was noted that although many methods have been proposed for mitigating leakage and misuse of relational data (some using anomaly detection and other using domain knowledge), none of the proposed methods considers the sensitivity level of the data to which the user may be exposed. Consequently, in [Harel, 2010], the *M-score (Misusability score)* measure was proposed, which estimates potential damage by measuring the sensitivity of the data that were exposed to the user. This measure is tailored for tabular datasets and is domain-dependent, meaning that it relies on a set of specific definitions provided by a domain expert. Collecting these data is the main challenge in applying the measure, especially in domains with a large number of attributes, each having many possible values. The measure incorporates four factors:

(1) Number of entities (quantity): this is the data size with respect to the different entities that appear in the data. Having data about more entities obviously increases the potential damage as a result of a misuse of these data.

(2) Number of properties: data can include a variety of details, or properties, on each entity (e.g., employee salary or patient disease). Because each additional property can increase the damage done as a result of a misuse, the number of different properties (i.e., the amount of information on each entity) should affect the misusability weighting.

(3) Values of properties (quality): the property value of an entity can greatly affect the misusability level of the data. For example, a patient record with a disease property equal to HIV should probably be more sensitive than a record concerning a patient with a simple flu.
(4) Anonymity level (distinguishing factor): although the number of different entities in the data can increase the misusability weight, the anonymity level of the data can decrease it. The anonymity level is regarded as the effort which is required to identify fully a specific entity in the data.

7.1.2.1   The M-score measure

The M-score is a measure used to estimate the extent of damage that a user can cause to an organization using the data that he or she encounters in the course of work [Harel, 2012]. This is done by ranking the sensitivity level of the data to which the user is exposed. Using this information, the organization can then take appropriate steps to prevent possible damage or to minimize its impact.

The M-score measure is tailored for tabular datasets (i.e., result sets of relational database queries) and is aimed at assigning a sensitivity score to a given set of tuples. It incorporates the following three factors:

- **Quality of the information**: the importance of the information to the organization.
- **Quantity of the information**: how much information is exposed.
- **Distinguishing factor**: the amount of effort required to identify the specific entities in the tuples.

To calculate the measure, three nonintersecting types of attributes are defined: identifier (or quasi-identifier) attributes; sensitive attributes; and other attributes, which are ignored in the calculation. The M-score measure is derived using the following formula:

$$MSCORE = r^{1/x} \times \max_{0 \le i \le r}\left(\frac{RRS_i}{D_i}\right) = r^{1/x} \times RS$$

where

r - the number of tuples in the published set, representing the quantity factor of the M-score;
RRS_i (*Raw Record Score*) - the sensitivity rank of the tuple i. This rank is assigned using a sensitivity-score function defined according to the domain expert's knowledge. The RRS_i component represents the quality factor;
D_i - a tuple i distinguishing factor, calculated by counting the number of entities with identical identifiers that exist in the organization's database;
RS (*Records Score*) - the maximum value of RRS_e/D_i; and
x - a settable parameter that defines the quality vs. quantity tradeoff. The domain expert needs to define the degree of importance of the published set size (r, which

Customer Name	Account Type
Anton Richter	Bronze
Otto Hecht	Gold

Table 7.1 A publication containing customer records

is an unbounded positive integer), compared to the sensitivity of the data in it (*RS*, which is a real number in the range of 0 to 1).

To demonstrate the calculation of the M-score, Table 7.1, which presents a published set of tuples containing customer data is used. Each tuple contains an identifier attribute (customer name) and a sensitive attribute (account type).

In this example, it is assumed that the sensitivity-score values of AccountType[Gold] and AccountType[Bronze] are 0.8 and 0.3 respectively. In addition, the company database contains only one customer with the name "Anton Richter," but 300 different customers with the name "Otto Hecht." Assuming $x = 1$ (i.e., every tuple leaked is highly sensitive) then the M-score measure of the publication can be calculated as follows:

$$MScore(\textbf{\textit{Table}}\ 1) = 2 \times \max_{0 \le i \le 2}\left(\frac{0.3}{1}, \frac{0.8}{300}\right) = 0.6$$

The misusability weight can be used to: (1) performed anomaly detection by learning the normal behavior of an insider in terms of the sensitivity level of the data to which she is usually exposed; (2) improve the process of handling leakage incidents identified by other misuse detection systems by enabling the security officer to focus on the incidents which involve more sensitive data; (3) implement a dynamic misusability-based access control protocol designed to regulate user access to sensitive data stored in relational databases [Harel, 2011a]; and (4) reduce the misusability of the data.

One of the main challenges in applying the M-score measure is acquiring the required knowledge needed to derive the sensitivity-score function. The sensitivity-score function assigns a sensitivity level to a given set of attribute values. Acquiring such a sensitivity-score function is a challenging task, especially in domains with a large number of attributes, each with many possible values. Harel *et al.* (2011b) describe an experiment conducted to evaluate two different approaches to acquiring the domain expert knowledge necessary to derive the sensitivity-score function. The experiment showed that the M-score achieves its goal of ranking the sensitivity level and expresses the domain expert's indications as to which data are more sensitive.

7.2 Using honeytokens

Honeytokens are artificial digital data items which are deliberately planted into a genuine system resource to detect unauthorized attempts to use information. Honeytokens are characterized by properties which make them appear to be genuine data items. Honeytokens are also accessible to potential attackers who intend to violate an organization's security in an attempt to mine information in a malicious manner. Depending on security needs, honeytokens are usually planted among real tokens in the database and are monitored to detect any associated activity associated. For example, a cellular phone company that is using the services of a third-party partner to market its new campaign to its customers can plant a "honey-customers" in the database which can be monitored to detect a partner who contacts customers with marketing materials other than those agreed upon. One of the main challenges in generating honeytokens is creating data items that appear real and that are difficult to distinguish from real tokens. Berkovitch *et al.* (2011) presented *"HoneyGen,"* a method for generating honeytokens automatically. HoneyGen creates honeytokens that are similar to real data by extrapolating the characteristics and properties of real data items. The input to HoneyGen includes a set of real tokens (genuine data items from the production environment) that are stored in a relational database consisting of one or more tables. No information about the attribute type, data domain, primary and foreign keys, or any other metadata is required. HoneyGen extrapolates rules that describe the "real" data structure, attributes, constraints and logic and then automatically generates artificial data items that comply with these rules and therefore appear to be "real." Afterwards, HoneyGen ranks the generated honeytokens according to their similarity to real tokens. The highest-ranked honeytokens can later be used as a simple and efficient security mechanism.

HoneyGen's honeytokens can be used as a simple and efficient security mechanism to detect intrusions, data misuse, and data leakage performed either by outsiders or by insiders. It is capable of automatically generating honeytokens for any type of data item (e.g., customer records, social network profiles, data sent over networks, patient medical files, etc.) as long as the data are stored in a tabular structure.

HoneyGen's honeytoken generation process consists of three main phases: rule mining, honeytoken generation and likelihood rating.

In the *rule mining* phase, the input database, containing real tokens, is used to extract various types of rules which characterize the real tokens. The rules are organized into five categories as defined by Duncan and Wells (1999): identity, reference, cardinal, value set, and attribute dependency rules. For example, for each attribute, several rules are defined to characterize the attribute type; a list of valid values (for discrete attributes) or value boundaries (for continuous attributes); relationships between records, and more.

Next, in the *honeytoken generation* phase, a method developed by Yahalom *et al.* (2010) for creating artificial relational databases is used. This method creates anonymous or artificial data for application testing based on a production database (real tokens) to enable organizations to outsource their testing processes to third parties without revealing sensitive information. As input, this method receives rules that describe the database constraints and transforms them into constraint satisfaction problems (CSPs). It is assumed that the organization provides these rules. One contribution of HoneyGen is therefore the development of an automated process for rule mining that can be provided to the artificial data generator presented in [Yahalom, 2010]. In this research the "generation" mode was used, in which artificial data are created from scratch, based only on the given rules (in other words, real tokens are not used for generating the honeytokens).

Finally, in the *likelihood rating* step, HoneyGen scores and sorts the honeytokens by calculating a rank for each honeytoken based on its similarity to the real tokens in the input database. A high rank indicates that the honeytoken consists of a combination of values that are common among real tokens and that therefore this honeytoken will likely appear to be real. Assume that there are n attributes in a schema, denoted by $a_1,...,a_{n-1},a_n$. For each attribute a_i, a probabilistic prediction model M_i (e.g., a classification and regression tree) is generated that, given the values of all other attributes, provides the conditional distribution $p(a_i | M_i, a_j, j=1,...,n, j \neq i)$. The models are generated using a training set containing real tokens.

Given the honeytoken tuple h, where $h = (v_1, v_2, .., v_n)$ and v_i is the value assigned to attribute a_i, the likelihood score of h is computed by using the trained models described above to compute the probability of the honeytoken's attribute values. The final likelihood score is derived by summing the logarithmic likelihood of all individual attributes:

$$L(h) = \sum_{i=1}^{n} \log \left(p \left(a_i = v_i \mid M_i; a_j = v_j, j = 1,...,n, j \neq i \right) \right)$$

The higher this rank, the more similar the honeytoken is to the real tokens, and therefore the harder it will be to identify it as an artificial entity. The final output of the HoneyGen process is a database with a structure identical to that of the input database in its structure and which contains artificial data items that are ranked according to their likelihood values.

To evaluate HoneyGen, a random sample of 1,093 publicly published profiles of women (extracted from a real dating website: okFreeDating.net) was used. The database consisted of 20 attributes representing the profile owner's personal information and 10 attributes describing the kind of partner in which the owner of the profile is interested. HoneyGen was used to generate 13,060 honeytokens that were also ranked according to their likelihood score.

As defined previously, a high-quality honeytoken is one that even an expert in the relevant domain will be unable to distinguish from a real token. Therefore, a Turing-like test was created to evaluate the quality of the honeytokens generated by HoneyGen. The authors developed a Web-based interactive pairwise experiment in which each participant was presented with 30 pairs of profiles (one pair at a time). Each pair consisted of one genuine profile and one honeytoken profile. The participant was asked to mark the profile that he or she believed was computer-generated (i.e., a honeytoken). The main goal of the experiment was to evaluate the quality of the generated honeytokens and the likelihood rating method. The main hypothesis is that honeytokens with a high likelihood rate can be detected with a probability of 50%, which is the probability that random selection would be expected to achieve. The 109 subjects who participated in this study included academic researchers (faculty members), information security specialists, graduate students, and undergraduate students from the

Department of Information Systems Engineering at Ben-Gurion University of the Negev in Israel. As expected, the results showed that honeytoken detection rates generally decreased as their likelihood ratio increased (they become more similar to the real tokens). The honeytoken detection rate confidence interval was (0.47, 0.67) with a confidence level of 0.95. Because this confidence interval includes the value 0.5 (i.e., a random detection rate), it can be concluded that the proposed likelihood-based criterion is a suitable means for selecting undetectable honeytokens.

7.3 Email leakage

Modern business activities rely extensively on email exchange. Various solutions attempt to analyze email exchange to prevent emails from being sent to the wrong recipients. However, there are still no satisfactory solutions. Addressing mistakes are not detected, and in some cases, correct recipients are wrongly marked as potential addressing mistakes.

As presented in Section 4.2.3, most current academic solutions which aim to prevent email leaks and are based on social interaction traffic analysis focus on analyzing the emails sent and received by an individual when an email is emanates from the individual's computer. These solutions provide accurate analysis in most cases, but there are cases in which analysis of emails sent and received by an individual in the past by itself is not enough to correctly classify a new email which the individual is about to send. For example, assume that the members of group G discuss topic T. Alice and Bob belong to G, but have never discussed topic T before (or even "worse," Alice and Bob have never communicated before). If Bob sends an email to Alice which contains content from topic T, current techniques may classify it by mistake as a potential leak.

Group email exchange analysis provides additional information about potential connections between users who discuss similar topics, but who do not necessarily communicate with each other. Thus, it better reflects the "real picture" of topics common to different users than simple analysis of an individual user's email exchanges with other users. Zilberman et al. (2010) presented a new approach to be used in organizations to prevent email leakage. The approach presented analyzes email exchanges among all members of the organization, extracts the topics discussed in the organization by email exchange, and derives groups of members which share the same topic. Consequently, each member may belong to several topic groups, and a topic group may contain members who have never communicated before. When a new email is composed, each recipient is classified either as a potential leak recipient or as a legitimate one. The classification is based not only on the emails exchanged between the sender and the recipient, but also on the topic groups to which they belong.

The proposed email leakage detection process consists of two phases: a training phase and a classification phase. The training is applied on a set of emails known to be leak-free, and the classification is applied on newly composed emails represented as queries. Let a query refer to an email with content c that is about to be sent from sender s to recipient r, and let the query be modeled as the triplet $\langle s,r,c \rangle$. Therefore, an email with x recipients defines x queries ($\langle s,r_1,c \rangle$, .., $\langle s,r_x,c \rangle$).

In the training phase, topic-oriented groups of users are identified based on the emails that they exchange (such that the members of each group exchange emails with similar content). This phase is divided into two main steps: (1) identifying, by clustering, the topics (cluster centroids) discussed in an organization; and (2) projection of the various topics onto the users. This process includes counting how many of each user's sent and received emails are associated with each topics.

In this field, as in many other areas of machine learning, a good distance metric is crucial for the success of the model. Moreover, emails usually contain short texts, which present an additional difficulty in representing and comparing emails. A technique called *context-based analysis* (*CoBAn*) [Katz, 2010] has been used for this purpose. CoBAn attempts to detect key terms and contexts using hierarchical language models which are an adaptation of frequently used language models. The CoBAn representation technique was compared with a baseline approach in which emails were represented as *TF-IDF* vectors and their similarity to the topic clusters was computed using a cosine measure [Zilberman, 2011].

During the testing phase, for each recipient of a given email, it is verified whether the recipient and the sender belong to at least one common topic group. If such a group does not exist, it may be concluded that there is no common topic for the two users to discuss and that the recipient is a wrong recipient. Otherwise, the content of the email is compared to the content of emails exchanged in each of the common groups. If the similarity score is high enough, the recipient may be considered as a legitimate recipient. For example, assume that Alice and Bob belong to the same group that exchanges on topic T and that Bob sends an email with content T to Alice. Alice will not be considered as a wrong recipient even if Alice and Bob have never directly exchanged emails with content T before.

The Enron email dataset[1] was used for evaluation. The Enron dataset contains 517,430 emails organized into 150 Enron-user folders. For the purposes of evaluation, the same 20 Enron-user folders that were used by Carvalho and Cohen (2007) were used. These folders contain 86,837 emails.

The dataset was split into training and testing sets. The older emails were used for training and the newer emails for testing. To the best of the authors' knowledge, there is no validated information regarding which of the emails' recipients in the Enron dataset represents an accidental or an intentional leakage. Therefore, it can be assumed that the original recipients of these emails are legitimate, although this may slightly compromise the results of the evaluation.

To evaluate the proposed method, for each email in the test set sent by user u, one randomly simulated recipient, who was not among the original recipients of the email, was "injected." There were two conditions for the inclusion of the false

---

[1] http://www.cs.cmu.edu/~enron/

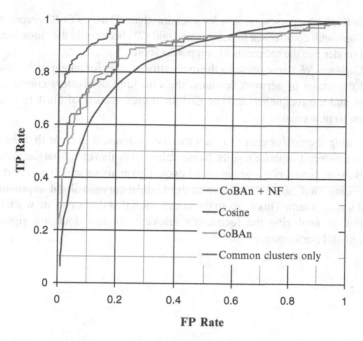

Fig. 7.3 Classifier evaluation results: TPR vs. FPR

recipient: (a) the recipient had to appear in the training set; and (b) the recipient had not received (in the training set) an email with the same subject as the email to which he or she was now assigned. The motivation behind this condition is to avoid simulating "leak" (false) recipients who in reality could be legitimate recipients. The classifier was then applied to each recipient, noth original and simulated. Evaluation results showed that a classifier model based on the new approach detected 90% of the potential leaks, but with false alarms for 20% of the legitimate recipients. However, it should be noted that half these alarms were raised for recipients who had no topic in common with the sender of the test email.

The results of the evaluation (true positive and false positive rates) are shown in Figure 7.3, where the y-axis represents the true positive rate (TPR), the percentage of "injected" recipients (i.e., wrong recipients) classified as leaks, and the x-axis represents the false positive rate (FPR), the percentage of legitimate recipients classified as leaks by mistake. Figure 7.3 shows four receiver operating characteristic (ROC) curves. Three of them, *CoBAn+NF*, *CoBAn*, and cosine present the TP and FP rates for different variations of the classification phase:

- The *cosine curve* presents a baseline version of the classification phase. In the baseline version, emails are represented as *TF-IDF* vectors, and their similarity to the clusters is computed using the cosine measure. Only the clusters common to the sender and the recipients are taken into account when computing the recipient's score.

- The *CoBAn curve* presents results for a version that: (1) uses a *CoBAn* representation of clusters with comparison to new emails; and (2) checks only the clusters common to the sender and the recipients to compute a score.
- The *CoBAn + NF curve* presents the evaluation results for an algorithm that combines the usage of network features, the checking of clusters common to the sender and the recipients, and the *CoBAn* representation of clusters with comparison to new emails.

Comparing the *cosine* curve to the other two curves, it is clear that the *CoBAn* technique produced superior results. Nonetheless, it is also clear that the main factor in the results achieved is the group email exchange analysis which was performed.

Comparing the *CoBAn + NF* curve to the *CoBAn* curve, a slight improvement in the results is apparent. This leads to the conclusion that the use of network features in addition to analyzing the recipient's relevant clusters does not significantly improve model performance.

Chapter 8
Future Trends in Data Leakage

This book provides a systematic study of the data leakage prevention domain. This study is based on a taxonomy that characterizes various aspects of the data leakage problem. An analysis of current industrial solutions and the research state of the art is presented.

From this study, it can be concluded that the DLP industry is very heterogeneous because it evolved out of the mature product lines of leading IT security vendors. A broad arsenal of enabling technologies, such as firewalls, encryption, access control, identity management, content/context-based detectors, and others, has already been incorporated to offer protection against various facets of the data-leakage threat. The competitive benefits of developing a "one-stop-shop," silver-bullet DLP suite reside mainly in the possibility of effectively orchestrating these enabling technologies to provide the highest degree of protection by ensuring an optimal fit of specific DLP technologies with the "threat landscape" in which they operate. This landscape is characterized by the types of leakage channels, data states, users, and IT platforms.

Designated commercial DLP solutions capable of monitoring DIM/DIU and scanning DAR can significantly reduce the risk of most accidental leakage scenarios. These solutions, however, do not provide sufficient protection against intentional leakage. Device control limits sensitive data exposure to external devices and also protects data when combined with a policy that enforces encryption. Protection from intentional leakage can be partially provided using a RMS access-control framework, which adds control over the data outside the organization, activity-based verification and authentication, anomaly detection (aimed at detecting data misuse), and honeypots.

Additional "non-designated" DLP solutions and measures include thin clients, workstation configuration management policies (e.g., preventing the installation of unapproved applications such as file sharing), anti-malware software, IDS, and firewalls. These also provide assistance in detecting malicious software or intrusion attempts and enforce policies that define a blueprint for protecting data, with the additional benefit of raising employee awareness. Technical measures include

A. Shabtai et al., *A Survey of Data Leakage Detection and Prevention Solutions*,
SpringerBriefs in Computer Science, DOI 10.1007/978-1-4614-2053-8_8,
© The Author(s) 2012

bundling laptops with encryption capabilities; two-factor authentication; ensuring that updated anti-malware utilities are installed; and preventing installation of unapproved applications. Administrative measures include directives that laptops should not be left unattended in cars; proper disposal of media; mandating strong passwords; and directives that passwords should never be stored near the computer and should never be passed to others.

Nevertheless, even such measures do not perfectly prevent or address intentional leaks. Research into innovative approaches such as activity-based verification, anomaly detection, improved content analysis methods (such as machine learning and statistical methods) that will be more resilient to content modifications, and honeypots should be further pursued to provide more effective solutions that will detect and block intentional leakage.

The authors conclude that future research in DLP should also focus on the following topics: accidental leakage by insiders and data leakage from mobile devices.

Accidental data leakage is addressed mainly by solutions that monitor traffic among users (within or outside the organization). The content of this traffic is compared to the organization's confidential information to detect any potential leakage. Future research should be directed to developing solutions that analyze the accidental leakage by users of non-sensitive pieces of information that may eventually be exploited by Web-based intelligence tools to derive confidential information about the organization. For example, assume there are rumors that a company is about to acquire another company. An adversary may try to derive which company is about to be acquired by carefully examining the Facebook accounts of relevant employees (for example, analysis of photos uploaded by the VP responsible for M&A from her last business trip). The publication of these pictures was a very serious information leakage performed by a member of the organization outside the organization's control. Providing solutions to such leakage scenarios is challenging.

Data misuse by insiders is expected to continue to be one of the most challenging research topics in the future. Recent incidents described in the book have demonstrated the huge damage that a few members of the organization can create. Detecting data misuse with reasonable false positive rate is very challenging because misusers are aware of the fact that the organization is monitoring their activities and may perform their malicious activities below the detection radar over a long period of time. In addition, data misusers in the future may be part of a larger attack in which their role will be mainly to activate an *advanced persistent threat* (APT) inside the organization. The APT will use vulnerability to collect and leak the confidential information. Detecting misusers that activate an APT is expected to be a future research challenge.

Mobile devices and particularly smartphones are expected to become the main computerized devices that members of the organization use and will use in the future. Because smartphones are used to access the organization's confidential data such as emails and documents, it is expected that they will be used to leak information accidently and intentionally. There have been several attempts to extend the organization's security perimeter into smartphones. There is a need for future research to find ways how on the one hand to allow members of the organizations to access confidential information through their smartphones, and on the other hand to prevent this information from leaking out of the smartphone intentionally or accidentally through malicious applications that the user downloaded from the mobile application markets. This future research is very challenging because smartphone include many communication channels (SMS, WIFI, 3 G, USB, BlueTooth, etc.) and monitoring them all is not easy. In addition, a smartphone cannot run complex detection algorithms because of its limited battery capacity and computational power.

References

Abbadi, I.M., and Alawneh, M. 2008. Preventing insider information leakage for enterprises. *Proceedings, International Conference on Emerging Security Information, Systems and Technologies*, 99–106.

Agrawal, R., Imieliniski, T., Swami, A. 1993. Mining association rules between sets of items in large databases. *SIGMOD Records* 22(2), 207–216.

Alawneh, M., and Abbadi, I.M. 2008. Preventing information leakage between collaborating organizations. *Proceedings, 10th International Conference on Electronic Commerce.*

Androutsopoulos, I., Koutsias, J., Cbandrinos, K.V., and Spyropoulos, C.D. 2000. An experimental comparison of naive Bayesian and keyword-based anti-spam filtering with personal e-mail messages. *Proceedings, 23rd Annual International ACM SIGIR Conference on Research and Development in Information Retrieval*, 160–167.

Bayardo, R.J., and Aggrawal, R. 2005. Data privacy through optimal k-anonymization. *Proceedings, 21st IEEE International Conference on Data Engineering (ICDE)*. Tokyo, Japan, 217–228.

Berkovich, M., Renford, M., Hansson, L., Shabtai, A., Rokach, L., and Elovici, Y. 2011. HoneyGen: an automated honeytokens generator, *Proceeding, IEEE Intelligence and Security Informatics (ISI 2011)*, Beijing, China, July 10–12, 2011

Borders, K., and Prakash, A. 2008. Towards quantification of network-based information leaks via HTTP. *Proceedings, 3rd conference on Hot Topics in Security.*

Bowen, B.M., Hershkop, S., Keromytis, A.D., and Stolfo, S.J. 2009a. Baiting inside attackers using decoy documents. *Proceedings, 5th International ICST Conference (SecureComm'09).*

Bowen, B.M., Salem M.B., Hershkop, S., Keromytis, A.D., and Stolfo, S.J. 2009b. Designing host and network sensors to mitigate the insider threat. *IEEE Security and Privacy*, 7(6), 22–29.

Bunker, G., and Gareth, F.K. 2009. *Data Leaks for Dummies*. Wiley.

Byers, S. 2004. Information leakage caused by hidden data in published documents. *IEEE Security and Privacy*, 2(2), 23–27.

Caputo D.D., Stephens G.D., and Maloof M.A. 2009. Detecting insider theft of trade secrets. *IEEE Security and Privacy*, 7(6), 14–21.

Carvalho, V.R., and Balasubramanyan, R. 2009. Information leaks and suggestions: a case study using Mozilla Thunderbird. *Proceedings, 6th Conference on Email and Anti-Spam.*

Carvalho, V.R., and Cohen, W. 2007. Preventing information leaks in email. *Proceedings, SIAM International Conference on Data Mining.*

Cathey, R., Ma, L., Goharian, N., and Grossman, D. 2003. Misuse detection for information retrieval systems. *Proceedings, 12th ACM Conference on Information and Knowledge Management (CIKM).*

Čenys, A., Rainys, D., Radvilavičius, L., and Goranin, N. 2005. Implementation of honeytoken module in DBMS Oracle 9iR2 Enterprise Edition for internal malicious activity detection.

A. Shabtai et al., *A Survey of Data Leakage Detection and Prevention Solutions*,
SpringerBriefs in Computer Science, DOI 10.1007/978-1-4614-2053-8,
© The Author(s) 2012

Proceedings, Conference on Detection of Intrusions and Malware & Vulnerability Assessment (DIMVA'05).

Chung, C.Y., Gertz, M., and Levitt, K. 1999. DEMIDS: A misuse detection system for database systems. Proceedings, *Conference on Integrity and Internal Control in Information Systems*, 159–178.

Cohen, W.W. 1996. Learning rules that classify e-mail. *Proceedings, AAAI Symposium on Machine Learning in Information Access*, 18–25.

Cohen, W.W., and Singer, Y. 1999. Context-sensitive learning methods for text categorization. *ACM Transactions on Information Systems (TOIS)*, 17(2), 11–17.

De Capitani di Vimercati, S., Foresti, S., Jajodia, S., Paraboschi, S., and Samarati, P. 2010. Encryption policies for regulating access to outsourced data. *ACM Transactions on Database Systems*, 35(2), 12:2–12:46.

Domingo-Ferrer, J. 2008. Privacy-Preserving Data Mining: Models and Algorithms. Springer, Chapter A Survey of Inference Control Methods for Privacy-Preserving Data Mining, 53–80.

Drucker, H., Wu, D., and Vapnik, V.N. 1999. Support vector machines for spam categorization. *IEEE Transactions on Neural Networks*, 10(5), 1048–1054.

Duncan, K., and Wells, D. 1999. Rule-based data cleansing. *Journal of Data Warehousing*, 4(3), 2–15.

Dwork, C. 2006. Differential privacy. *Proceedings, 33rd International Colloquium on Automata, Languages and Programming (ICALP)*. Venice, Italy, 1–12.

Elovici Y, Rokach, L., and Albayrak S. 2012. Special issue on Data Mining for Information Security, *Information Sciences*.

Fonseca, J., Vieira, M., and Madeira, H. 2008. Online detection of malicious data access using DBMS auditing. *Proceedings, 2008 ACM Symposium on Applied Computing*, 1013–1020.

Forte, D. 2009. Do encrypted disks spell the end of forensics? *Computer Fraud and Security*, 2009(2), 18–20.

Franqueira,V., Cleeff, A., Eck, P., and Wieringa, R. 2010. External insider threat: a real security challenge in enterprise value webs. *Proceedings, 5th International Conference on Availability, Reliability and Security*, 446–453.

Friedman, A., Wolff, R., and Schuster, A. 2009. Providing *k*-anonymity in data mining. *The International Journal on Very Large Data Bases*, 17(4), 789–804.

Frost & Sullivan. 2008. *World Data Leakage Prevention Market*. Technical Report ND34D-74, Frost & Sullivan, United States.

Fung, B.C.M., Wang, K., and Yu, P.S. 2005. Top-down specialization for information and privacy preservation. *Proceedings, 21st IEEE International Conference on Data Engineering (ICDE)*, Tokyo, Japan, 205–216.

Fung, B.C.M., Wang, K., and Yu, P.S. 2007. Anonymizing classification data for privacy preservation. *IEEE Transactions on Knowledge and Data Engineering (TKDE)* 19(5), 711–725.

Fung, B., Wang, K., Fu, A., and Pei, J. 2008. Anonymity for continuous data publishing. *Proceedings, 11th International Conference on Extending Database Technology: Advances in Database Technology*. ACM, 264–275.

Fung, B., Wang, K., Chen, R., and Yu, P. 2010. Privacy-preserving data publishing: A survey of recent developments. *ACM Computing Surveys (CSUR)* 42(4), 1–53.

Gafny, M., Shabtai, A., Rokach, L., and Elovici, Y. 2011. Applying unsupervised context-based analysis for detecting unauthorized data disclosure. *Proceedings, ACM CCS* Chicago, USA, October 17–21, 2011.

Gaonjur, P., and Bokhoree, C. 2006. Risk of insider threats in information technology outsourcing: can deceptive techniques be applied? *Journal of Security and Management*, 522–529.

Gionis, A., Mazza, A. and Tassa, T. 2008. *k*-anonymization revisited. Proceedings, *International Conference on Data Engineering (ICDE)*, 744–753.

Gionis, A., Tassa, T. 2009. *k*-anonymization with minimal loss of information. *IEEE Transactions on Knowledge and Data Engineering*, 21, 206–219.

Goharian, N., Ma, L., and Meyers, C. 2005. Detecting misuse of information retrieval systems using data mining techniques (poster). *Proceedings, IEEE International Conference on Intelligence and Security Informatics*.

Goldberger, J. and Tassa, T. 2010. Efficient anonymizations with enhanced utility. *Transactions on Data Privacy* 3, 149–175.

Gritzalis, S. Acquisti, A. 2008. Digital privacy: theory, technologies, and practices. Auerbach Publications, Vol. 9 "Privacy Protection with Uncertainty and Indistinguishability."

Guha, S., Rastogi, R., and Shim, K. 2000. Rock: A Robust Clustering Algorithm for Categorical Attributes. *Information Systems*, 25(5), 345–366.

Hackle, A., and Hauer, B. 2009. State of the art in network relate extrusion prevention systems. *Proceedings, 7th International Symposium on Database Engineering and Applications*, pp. 329–335.

Harel, A., Shabtai, A., Rokach, L., and Elovici Y. 2010. M-score: estimating the potential damage of data leakage incident by assigning misuseability weight. *Proceedings, 2010 ACM workshop on Insider threats*.

Harel, A., Shabtai, A., Rokach, L., and Elovici Y. 2011a. Dynamic sensitivity-based access control. *Proceedings, IEEE Intelligence and Security Informatics (ISI 2011)*, Beijing, China, July 10–12, 2011.

Harel, A., Shabtai, A., Rokach, L., and Elovici Y. 2011b. Preventing data misuse: eliciting domain expert misusability conceptions. *Proceeding, 6th International Conference on Knowledge Capture (K-CAP 2011)*, Banff, Canada, June 26–29, 2011.

Harel, A., Shabtai, A., Rokach, L., and Elovici Y. 2012. M-Score: Estimating the Potential Damage of Data Leakage Incident by Assigning Misuseability Weight. *IEEE Transactions on Dependable and Secure Computing*.

Helfman, J., and Isbell, C. 1995. *Ishmail: Immediate Identification of Important Information*. Technical Report, AT&T Labs.

Hong, J., Kim, J., and Cho, J. 2010. The trend of the security research for the insider cyber threat. *International Journal of Future Generation Communication and Networking*, 3(2), 31–40.

Hovold, J. 2005. Naive Bayes span filtering using word-position-based attributes. *Proceedings, 2nd Conference on Email and Anti-Spam*.

Hu, Y., and Panda, B. 2004. A data mining approach for database intrusion detection. *Proceedings, 2004 ACM symposium on Applied computing*, pp. 711–716.

Hu, Y., and Panda, B. 2003. Identification of malicious transactions in database systems. *Proceedings, 7th International Symposium on Database Engineering and Applications*, pp. 329–335.

Hundepool, A., and Willenborg, L. 1996. mu- and tau-ARGUS: software for statistical disclosure control. *Proceedings, 3rd International Seminar on Statistical Confidentiality*.

Iyengar, V.S. 2002. Transforming data to satisfy privacy constraints. *Proceedings, 8th ACM SIGKDD*. Edmonton, AB, Canada, 279–288.

Kalyan, C., and Chandrasekaran, K. 2007. Information leak detection in financial emails using mail pattern analysis under partial information. *Proceedings, 7th Conference on 7th WSEAS International Conference on Applied Informatics and Communications*, 104–109.

Kamra, A., Terzi, E., Evimaria, and Bertino, E. 2008. Detecting anomalous access patterns in relational databases. *International Journal on Very Large Databases*, 17(5), 1063–1077.

Kabra, G., Ramamurthy, R., and Sudarshan, S. 2006. Redundancy and information leakage in fine-grained access control. *Proceedings, 2006 ACM SIGMOD international conference on Management of data*.

Katz, G., Elovici, Y., and Shapira, B. 2011. A new model for data leakage prevention. Submitted to *ACM Transactions on Information and System Security (TISSEC)*, January 10, 2011.

Kisilevich, S., Rokach, L., Elovici, Y., and Shapira, B. 2010. Efficient multidimensional suppression for k-anonymity. *IEEE Transactions on Knowledge and Data Engineering*, 22(3), 334–347.

Lawton, G. 2008. New technology prevents data leakage. *Computer*, 41(9), 14–17.

Lee, S.Y., Low, W.L. and Wong, P.Y. 2002. Learning fingerprints for a database intrusion detection system. *ESORICS*, 2502/2002, 264–279.

Lee, V., Stankovic, J.A., and Son, S.H. 2000. Intrusion detection in real-time database systems via time signatures. *Proceedings, 6th IEEE Real Time Technology and Applications Symposium*.

Lefevre, K., Dewitt, D. J., and Ramakrishnan, R. 2005. Incognito: efficient full-domain *k*-anonymity. *Proceedings, of ACM SIGMOD*. Baltimore, ML, 49–60.

Lefevre, K., Dewitt, D. J., and Ramakrishnan, R. 2006. Mondrian multidimensional *k*-anonymity. *Proceedings, 22nd IEEE International Conference on Data Engineering (ICDE)*. Atlanta, GA.

Ma, L., and Goharian, N. 2005. Query length impact on misuse detection in information retrieval systems. *Proceedings, ACM Symposium on Applied Computing*, 1070–1075.

Machanavajjhala, A., Gehrke, J., Kiferl, D., and Venkitasubramaniam, M. 2006. *l*-diversity: Privacy beyond *k*-anonymity. *Proceedings, the 22nd IEEE International Conference on Data Engineering (ICDE)*. Atlanta, GA.

Maybury, M., *et al*. 2005. Analysis and detection of malicious insiders. *Proceedings, 2005 International Conference on Intelligence Analysis*.

Menahem, E., Shabtai, A., Rokach, L., and Elovici, Y. 2009. Improving malware detection by applying multi-inducer ensemble. *Computational Statistics and Data Analysis*, 53(4), 1483–1494.

Mogull, R. 2007. *Understanding and Selecting a Data Loss Prevention Solution*. Technical Report, SANS Institute, Securosis.

Mun, H., Han, K., Yeun, C.Y., and Kim, K. 2008. Yet another intrusion detection system against Insider Attacks. *Proceesings, Symposium on Cryptography and Information Security*.

Nergiz, M. E. and Clifton, C. 2006. Thoughts on *k*-anonymization. *Proceedings, International Conference on Data Engineering (ICDE) Workshops*.

Nergiz, M.E., Clifton, C., and Nergiz, A.E. 2007. Multirelational *k*-anonymity. *Proceedings, 23rd International Conference on Data Engineering (ICDE)*. Istanbul, Turkey, 1417–1421.

NIST. 1995. *An Introduction to Computer Security: The NIST Handbook*.

Ouellet, E., and Proctor, P.E. 2009. *Magic Quadrant for Content-Aware Data Loss Prevention*. Technical Report, RA4 06242010, Gartner RAS Core Research.

Papadimitriou, P. and Garcia-Molina, H. 2010. Data leakage detection. *IEEE Transactions on Knowledge and Data Engineering*, pp. 51–63.

Parno, B., McCune, J.M., Wendlandt, D., Andersen, D.G., and Perrig, A. 2009. CLAMP: practical prevention of large-scale data leaks. *Proceedings, IEEE Symposium on Security and Privacy*.

Phua, C. 2009. Protecting organizations from personal data breaches. *Computer Fraud & Security*, 2009(2), 13–18.

Raschke, T. 2008. *The Forrester Wave™: Data Leak Prevention, Q2 2008*. Technical report, Forrester Research, Inc.

Rennie, J. 2000. ifile: an application of machine learning to e-mail filtering. *Proceedings, KDD-Workshop on Text Mining*.

Sahami, M., Dumais, S., Heckerman, D., and Horvitz, E. 1998. A Bayesian approach to filtering junk email. *AAAI-98 Workshop on Learning for Text Categorization*.

Salem, B.M., Heshkop, S., and Stolfo, S.J. 2008. A survey of insider attack detection eesearch. *Insider Attack and Cyber Security- Beyond the Hacker*, Springer, 39, 23–27.

Salem, B.M., and Stolfo, S.J. 2011a. Modeling user search behavior for masquerade detection. *Proceedings, 14th Proceedings of the Fourteenth Symposium on Recent Advances in Intrusion Detection (RAID 2011)*.

Salem, B.M., and Stolfo, S.J. 2011b. Decoy document deployment for effective masquerade attack detection. *Proceedings, 8th Conference on Detection of Intrusions and Malware & Vulnerability Assessment (DIMVA)*, pp. 35–54.

Salton, G., and McGill, M.J. 1986. *Introduction to Modern Information Retrieval*. McGraw-Hill, Inc., New York, USA.

Samarati, P. 2001. Protecting respondents' identities in microdata release. *IEEE Transactions on Knowledge and Data Engineering (TKDE)* 13(6), 1010–1027.

Samarati, P., and Sweeney, L. 1998. Generalizing data to provide anonymity when disclosing information. *Proceedings, 17th ACM SIGACT-SIGMOD-SIGART PODS*. Seattle, WA, 188.

Schenker, A. 2003. *Graph-Theoretic Techniques for Web Content Mining*. PhD thesis, University of South Florida.

Sharkey, P., Tian, H., Zhang W., and Xu, S., 2008. Privacy-Preserving Data Mining Through Knowledge Model Sharing. *Privacy, Security and Trust in KDD*, 4890, 97–115.

Shmueli, E., Tassa, T., Wasserstein, R., Shapira, B., and Rokach, L., 2012. Limiting Disclosure of Sensitive Data in Sequential Releases of Databases. *Information Sciences*.

Spalka, E., and Lehnhardt, J. 2005. A comprehensive approach to anomaly detection in relational databases. *Annual Working Conference on Data and Applications Security*, 3654/2005, 207–211.

Spitzner, L. 2003. Honeypots: catching the insider threat. *Proceedings, 19th Annual Computer Security Applications Conference (ACSAC'03)*, 170–179.

Srivastava, A., Sural, S., and Majumdar, A.K. 2006. Database intrusion detection using weighted sequence mining. *Journal of Computers*, 1(4), 8–17.

Stalling, W., and Brown, L. 2007. *Computer Security: Principles and Practice*, first ed. Prentice Hall.

Stolfo, S.J., Hershkop, S., Hu, C.W., Li, W.J., Nimeskern, O., and Wang, K. 2006. Behavior-based modeling and its application to Email analysis. *ACM Transactions Internet Technology*, 6(2), 187–221.

Storey, D. 2009. Catching flies with honey tokens. *Network Security*, 2009(11), 15–18.

Sunu, M., Michalis, P., Hung, N., and Shambhu, U. 2009. *A Data-Centric Approach to Insider Attack Detection in Database Systems*. Technical Report.

Sweeney, L. 1997. Datafly: a system for providing anonymity in medical data. In *Proceedings of the IFIP TC11 WG11.3 11th International Conference on Database Security XI: Status and Prospects*, 356–381.

Sweeney, L. 2002a. Achieving *k*-anonymity privacy protection using generalization and suppression. *International Journal on Uncertainty, Fuzziness, and Knowledge-based Systems* 10(5), 571–588.

Sweeney, L. 2002b. *k*-anonymity: a model for protecting privacy. *International Journal on Uncertainty, Fuzziness and Knowledge-based Systems*. 10, 557–570.

Valeur, F., Mutz, D., and Vigna, G. 2005. A learning-based approach to the detection of SQL attacks. *Proceedings, 14th Conference on Detection of Intrusions and Malware and Vulnerability Assessment (DIMVA)*, Vienna, Austria.

Valli, C. 2005. Honeypot technologies and their applicability as a strategic internal countermeasure. *International Journal of Information and Computer Security*, 1(4), 30–436.

Verykios, V.S., Bertino, E., Fovino, I.N., Provenza, L.P., Saygin, Y. and Theodoridis, Y. 2004. State-of-the-art in privacy preserving data mining. *ACM SIGMOD Record*, 33(1), 50–57.

Wang, K., Yu, P., and Chakraborty, S., 2004. Bottom-up generalization: a data mining solution to privacy protection. *Proceedings, 4th International Conference on Data Mining (ICDM'04)*, Brighton, U.K.

Wang, K., Fung, B., and Yu, P. 2005. Template-based privacy preservation in classication problems. Proceedings, *Fifth IEEE International Conference on Data Mining*.

Wang, K., and Fung, B.C.M. 2006. Anonymizing sequential releases. *Proceedings 12th ACM SIGKDD*. Philadelphia, PA.

Wenhui, S., and Tan, D. 2001. A novel intrusion detection system model for securing web-based database systems. *Proceedings, 25th IEEE International Computer Software and Applications Conference on Invigorating Software Development*.

White, J. 2010. Creating personally identifiable honeytokens. *Innovations and Advances in Computer Sciences and Engineering*, 227–232.

White, J., and Panda, B. 2009. Automatic identification of critical data items in a database to mitigate the effects of malicious insiders. *Proceedings, 5th International Conference on Information Systems Security*, 208–221.

White, J., and Panda, B. 2010. Insider threat discovery using automatic detection of mission critical data based on content. *Proceedings, Sixth International Conference on Information Assurance and Security (IAS)*, IEEE, pp. 56–61.

Wong, R.C.W., Li., J., Fu, A.W.C., and Wang, K. 2006. (α,k)-anonymity: An enhanced *k*-anonymity model for privacy preserving data publishing. *Proceedings, 12th ACM SIGKDD*. Philadelphia, PA, 754–759.

Xu, J., Wang, W., Pei, J., Wang, X., Shi, B., and Fu, A. W.C. 2006. Utility-based anonymization using local recoding. *Proceedings, 12th ACM SIGKDD Conference*. Philadelphia, PA.

Yahalom, R., Shmueli, E., and Zrihen, T. 2010. Constrained anonymization of production data: a constraint satisfaction problem approach. *Secure Data Management*, pp. 41–53.

Yao, C., Wang, X.S., and Jajodia, S. 2005. Checking for *k*-anonymity violation by views. *Proceedings, 31st Very Large Data Bases (VLDB)*. Trondheim, Norway, 910–921.

Yaseen, Q., and Panda, B. 2009. Knowledge acquisition and insider threat prediction in relational database systems. *Proceedings, 12th International IEEE Conference on Computational Science and Engineering*, 450–455.

Yasuhiro, K., and Yoshiki, S. 2002. A Web-based system for prevention of information leakage (poster). Proceedings, *11th International World Wide Web (WWW) Conference*.

Yixiang, S., Tao, P., and Minghua, J. 2007. Secure multiple XML documents publishing without information leakage. *Proceedings, International Conference on Convergence Information Technology*, 2114–2119.

Zhang, Q., Koudas, N., Srivastava, D., and Yu, T. 2007. Aggregate query answering on anonymized tables. In *Proceedings of the 23rd IEEE International Conference on Data Engineering (ICDE)*.

Zhu, H., Shi, J., Wang, Y., and Feng, Y., 2008. Controlling Information Leakage of Fine-grained Access model in DBMSs, In *Proceedings of the 9th International Conference on Web-Age Information Management*, 583–590.

Zilberman, P., Katz., G., Elovici, Y., Shabtai, A. and Dolev, S., 2011. Analyzing group communication for preventing data leakage via email. *Proceedings, IEEE Intelligence and Security Informatics (ISI 2011)*, Beijing, China, July 10–12, 2011.

Zilberman, P., Shabtai, A., Rokach, L. 2010. Analyzing group communication for preventing accidental data leakage via email. *Proceedings, Workshop on Collaborative Methods for Security and Privacy (CollSec 2010)*, Washington DC, USA, August 10, 2010.